Making Places

Hands-On Lessons for Learning Phonics, Spelling, and Geography

Patricia M. Cunningham

Carson-Dellosa Publishing Company, Inc.
Greensboro, NC

Credits

Editors
Michelle DeWitt
Joey Bland

Layout Design
Jon Nawrocik

Inside Illustrations
Mike Duggins

Cover Design
Matthew VanZomeren

Table of Contents

Table of Contents

Table of Contents

Introduction

Since the publication of *Making Words,* which Dottie Hall and I wrote in 1994 (Good Apple), teachers and children have enjoyed this hands-on, concrete way to learn how to decode and spell words. In this book, I extend this enjoyable activity to teach not only phonics and spelling, but also geography. Recent surveys put American children near the bottom of the developed nations in their knowledge of geography. This book provides 160 lessons in which each secret word or phrase is the name of a geographical place. In addition to the secret place, each lesson contains as many other place names as possible; this way, places that don't have enough letters to be a secret place are also included.

In addition to teaching geography, these lessons also teach children important information about phonics and spelling. As children manipulate the letters to make the words, they learn how small changes, such as changing one letter or moving the letters around, result in completely new words. Children learn to stretch out words and listen for the sounds they hear and the order of those sounds. Children also learn that when you change the first letter, you also change the sound you hear at the beginning of the word. Likewise, when you change the last letter, you change the sound you hear at the end of the word. These ideas seem commonplace and obvious to those of us who have been reading and writing for almost as long as we can remember. But, they are a revelation to many beginners—a revelation that gives them tremendous independence in and power over the challenge of decoding and spelling words.

Making Words lessons are an example of a type of instruction called "guided discovery." In order to truly learn and retain strategies, children must discover them. But, some children do not seem to make discoveries about words very easily on their own. In a Making Words lesson, the teacher guides students toward those discoveries by carefully sequencing the words they will make and giving them explicit guidance about how much change is needed.

Step One: Making Words

Each *Making Places* lesson begins with short, easy words and builds to longer, more complex words, including the secret place that can be made with all of the letters. As children make a word at their desks, a child who has it made successfully goes up to the pocket chart or overhead projector and makes the word with big letters. Children who didn't make the word correctly quickly fix it to be ready for the next word. The small changes between most words in the lesson encourage even those children who have not made a word perfectly to fix it. They soon realize that having the current word correctly spelled increases their chances of spelling the next word correctly. In each lesson, the teacher and students make 9–15 words, including the secret place that can be made with all of the letters. When it is time to make the secret place, the teacher gives children one minute to try to come up with the word. After one minute, if no one has discovered the secret place, the teacher gives children clues that allow them to figure it out.

Step Two: Sorting the Words into Patterns

Many children discover patterns just through making the words in the carefully sequenced order, but some children need more explicit guidance. This guidance happens when all of the words have been made and the teacher guides children to sort the words into patterns.

One pattern that children need to discover is that many words have the same root word. If they can pronounce and spell the root word and if they recognize root words with endings, prefixes, or suffixes added, they are able to decode and spell many additional words. To some children, every new word they meet is a new experience! They fail to recognize how new words are related to already known words and thus are in the difficult—if not impossible—position of starting from "scratch" and just trying to learn and remember every new word. To be fluent, fast, automatic decoders and spellers, children must learn that **act**, **active**, **inactive**, and **actively** have **act** as their root. They must also use their knowledge of how to decode and spell **act** to quickly transfer to these related words. Whenever possible, *Making Places* lessons include related words using the letters available. The teacher tells children that people are related by blood and words are related by meaning. The teacher asks children to find any related words and sort them, then she creates sentences to show how these words are related. For example: When we **act**, we do something. An **active** person does a lot of things. **Inactive** people don't do very much. The candidates for school board **actively** sought voters.

In every *Making Places* lesson, the teacher and students sort the rhyming words. There are several sets of rhyming words in each lesson. Children need to recognize that words that have the same spelling pattern from the vowel to the end of the word usually rhyme. Unlike Spanish, in which one letter has one sound, the sounds of many letters in English are determined by the letters that follow them. The vowel **a**, for example, has what are commonly called long and short sounds—in words like **cake** and **can**. It has very different sounds in words such as **saw**, **park**, **all**, **talk**, **laugh**, **usual**, and **mama**. In other words, such as **fear**, **said**, and **coat**, the letter **a** has no sound at all. To add to the confusion, some words, such as **weight**, have the long sound of **a** but no letter **a**!

English—and especially the vowels in English—simply cannot be explained based on individual letters. But, if you look at the spelling patterns—the vowels and the letters that follow them—English makes sense. All of the words that end in **a-k-e**, including **make**, **flake**, **snake**, and **earthquake**, rhyme with **cake**. All of the words that end in **a-l-l**, including **tall**, **small**, and **recall**, rhyme with **all**. When children sort words into rhyming words and notice that the words that rhyme have the same spelling pattern, they learn rhyming patterns and how to use words they know to decode and spell lots of other words.

Step Three: Transfer to Reading and Writing

All of the working and playing with words is worth nothing if children do not use what they know when they need to use it. Many children know letter sounds and patterns and do not apply these to decode unknown words encountered during reading or to spell words they need while writing. All teachers know that it is much easier to teach children phonics than it is to actually get them to use it. This is the reason that every *Making Places* lesson ends with a transfer step. Once words are sorted according to rhyme, the teacher tells children to pretend they are reading and come to a new word. As the teacher says this, she writes a word that has the same spelling pattern and rhymes with one set of rhyming words. The teacher shows this word to a child and asks him to come up and put the new word with the words it rhymes with. The teacher doesn't allow anyone to say the new word until it is lined up under the other rhyming words. She leads children to pronounce the rhyming words they made and the new word. Then, the teacher shows them one more word and says to a child: "Pretend you're reading and come to this new word. Put it with the words that would help you figure it out."

In *Making Places*, most of the transfer words have more than one syllable. The last syllable rhymes with the rhyming words children make. By using bigger words as transfer words, children can begin to recognize patterns they know in longer words.

Once students have decoded two new words using the rhyming patterns from the words they made, the teacher helps children transfer their letter-sound knowledge to writing. To do this, the teacher asks children to pretend they are writing and need to spell a word:

"Pretend you're writing and you need to spell the word **complain**. If you can think of the words we made today that rhyme with **the last syllable of complain**, you will have the correct spelling of the end of the word."

The children decide that the last syllable of **complain** rhymes with the words they made—**rain** and **gain**—and that the last syllable is spelled **p-l-a-i-n**. The teacher then helps them spell the first part of that word if that help is needed. Each *Making Places* lesson ends with children using the rhyming words they made to spell the last syllable of two other words. Children learn that rhyming patterns they know can help them spell both short words that rhyme and longer words in which the last syllables rhyme.

Setup

As the person who is teaching the lesson, you, the teacher, are always the best person to decide exactly what to say to your students and how to cue them about the different words. If you are teaching in Colorado and one of the words they make is **Denver**, you will cue them differently than a teacher whose school is in Florida. Your children will relate better to example sentences you come up with that relate to their communities and lives. With the caveat that you can do this much better for your students than I—who have never seen your children—can, here is a sample that you can use to construct your own lesson cues.

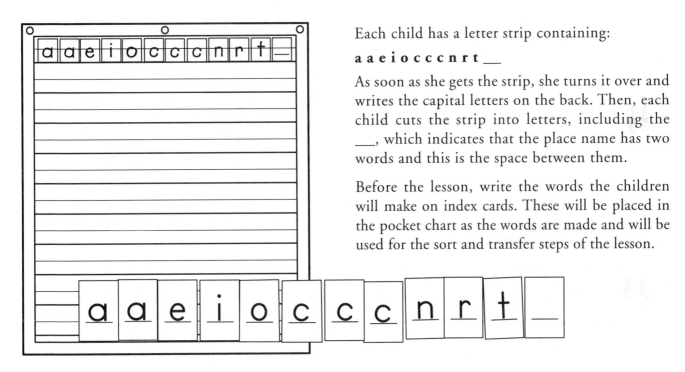

Each child has a letter strip containing:

a a e i o c c c n r t __

As soon as she gets the strip, she turns it over and writes the capital letters on the back. Then, each child cuts the strip into letters, including the __, which indicates that the place name has two words and this is the space between them.

Before the lesson, write the words the children will make on index cards. These will be placed in the pocket chart as the words are made and will be used for the sort and transfer steps of the lesson.

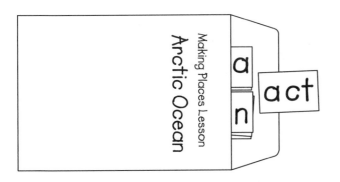

Begin the lesson by reminding students what the space means: "This place name is made up of two words." Also, make sure that classroom maps are displayed so that the secret place—and any other place words—can be located on the maps.

Ask everyone to begin with the letters showing their lowercase sides. Remind them that specific names—people and places—require that the first letters show the capital forms they just printed on the backs. Cue them to begin making words. The pace should be brisk. As each word is made, send someone to make it with the big letters in the pocket chart.

Step One: Making Words

"Use three letters to spell the word **act**. Juan likes to **act** in plays."

(Find a student with **act** spelled correctly and send that student to spell **act** with the big letters.)

"Good, now change just one letter to spell **ace**. In most card games, the **ace** is the highest card."

(Quickly send someone with the correct spelling to the big letters. Keep the pace brisk. Do not wait until everyone has **ace** spelled with his little letters. It is fine if some students are making **ace** as **ace** is being spelled with the big letters.)

"Change one letter again to spell **ice**. Do you like **ice** in your soda?"

(Continue sending students to make the words with the big letters. Remind everyone to use the big letters to check what they have made with their letters, fixing each word as needed before going on to the next word. Move the lesson along at a fast pace.)

"Add a letter to **ice** to spell **nice**."

"Change a letter in **nice** to spell **rice**."

"Change a letter again to turn **rice** into **race**. The fastest runner won the **race**."

(When children are not just adding or changing one letter, cue them to start over.)

"Start over and use 5 new letters to spell **ocean**. I love to swim in the **ocean**."

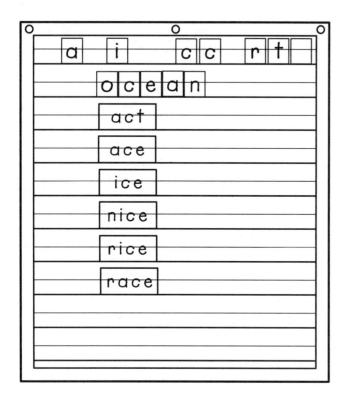

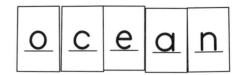

"Use the same letters in **ocean** to spell **canoe**. We **canoe** at the lake."

"Start over and use 5 new letters to spell **arena**. The game was in the new **arena**."

"Start over and use 5 new letters to spell **react**. I worried about how my mom would **react** to my report card."

"Use 6 letters to spell **action**. I wonder if they really say, 'Lights, camera, **action**!' when they direct movies."

Making Places • CD-104108 • © Carson-Dellosa

"Use 7 letters to spell **concert**. Did you go to the **concert** in the park on Sunday?"

(Always alert children when they are making a name and expect them to use a capital letter.)

"Take 7 letters and spell the country of **Croatia**. **Croatia** is a country in eastern Europe."

(Have someone locate **Croatia** on a map while the word is being made with the big letters.)

"This is the next-to-the-last word. Start over and use 8 letters to spell **reaction**. Everyone waited to see her **reaction** to the news that she had won the contest."

"I have just one word left. It is the secret place—a phrase you can make with all of your letters. Remember, it has two words in its name. See if you can figure it out."

(Give them one minute to figure out the secret place and then give clues if needed.)

"Our secret place is an ocean with 2 words in its name."

Let someone go to the big letters and spell the secret place—**Arctic Ocean**. Have the **Arctic Ocean** located on a map. Discuss its location and let students share anything they know about it.

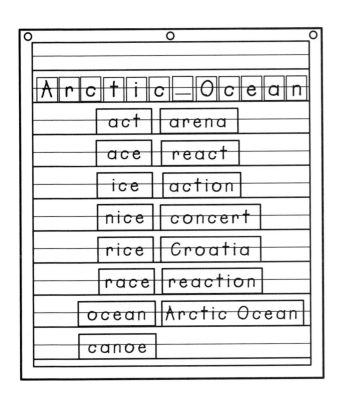

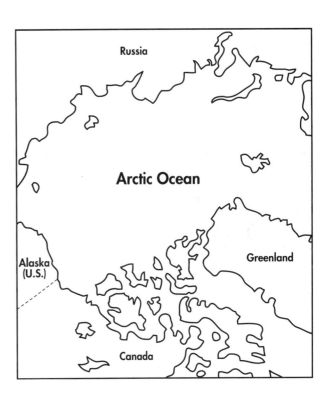

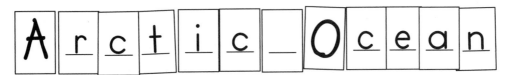

Step Two: Sorting the Words into Patterns

Have students read aloud with you all of the words made in the lesson. Then, ask someone to go to the pocket chart and pull out any related words. Remind children that words are related when they share the same root word and share some meaning.

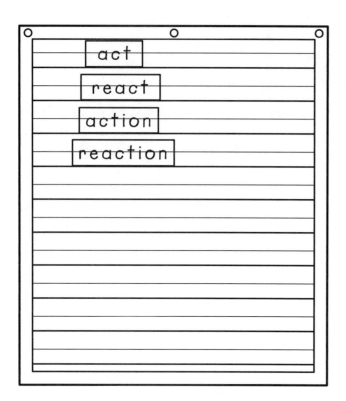

Sort Related Words

Have students make up sentences to show how the words are related. Model some sentences if necessary.

"People **act** in the movies, and they call this **action**."

"Sometimes, you **act** in a certain way and other people **react** in a different way."

"The way you react is your **reaction**."

"If you **act** bad, expect a bad **reaction**!"

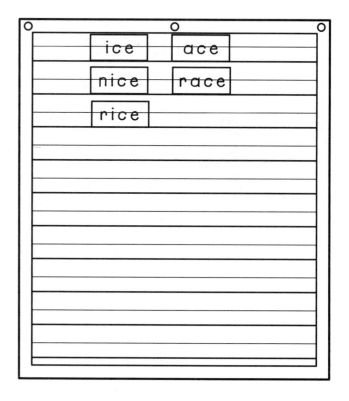

Sort Rhymes

Send someone to the pocket chart to find rhyming words with the same pattern and place the rhymes in columns. Have everyone pronounce the sets of rhymes and agree that they rhyme.

Making Places • CD-104108 • © Carson-Dellosa

Reading Transfer

Tell students to pretend they are reading and come to a new word. Show one person the word **sacrifice** written on an index card. Let that person put **sacrifice** under **ice**, **nice**, and **rice** and have all of the children pronounce all four words, making the last syllable rhyme with **ice**, **rice**, and **nice**. Do the same thing with **replace**.

Writing Transfer

Tell students to pretend they are writing and need to spell a word.

"Let's pretend Carla is writing and she is trying to spell the word **advice**."

Help students spell the first part and write **ad** on an index card. Then, have the children pronounce the sets of rhyming words in the pocket chart and decide that the last syllable of **advice** rhymes with **ice**, **nice**, and **rice**. Use the **i-c-e** pattern to finish spelling **advice** on the index card.

Do the same thing with **fireplace**.

When you finish the lesson, the rhyming words you made will be lined up in the pocket chart, along with the two new words students helped you read and the two new words they helped you spell.

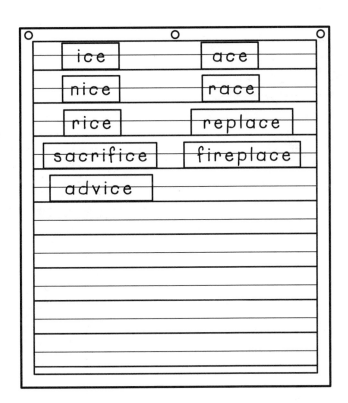

Because students like to manipulate the letters and come up with their own words, I usually give them a take-home sheet with the same letters used in the lesson. (See page 239 for the reproducible *Making Places* Take-Home Sheet.) The sheet has spaces for the letters across the top and blocks for writing words. Students write capital letters on the back and then cut the letters apart. They manipulate the letters to make words and then write them in the blocks. This is a popular homework assignment with students and their parents. When you write the letters at the top, write them in alphabetical order—vowels, then consonants—so as not to give away the secret place. Remember to use ___ (underline) when necessary to indicate a space between words and commas as needed. Before children take the sheets home, have them turn it over and write the capital letters on the backs. Children love being the "smart" ones who "know the secret place," and they love watching parents and other relatives try to figure it out.

Making Places Take-Home Sheet		
a a e i o c c c n r t _		

There are 160 *Making Places* lessons in this book. All of the secret words and phrases are places—most are specific places. We often call these specific places "proper nouns." It makes a lot more sense to children to call them "specific nouns." In order to contrast the specific place names with general ones, I have included some general (common) place nouns. You will find lessons in which the secret places are **nations**, **countries**, **continents**, **states**, **islands**, **mountains**, and **provinces**. These place names are general names and, unlike all of the specific names, do not have capital letters.

All of the states in the United States are represented in the lessons. Most of them are secret places, but some states' names were too short to generate enough words. In those cases, I have used the states and their capitals as the secret places: **Albany, New York**; **Augusta, Maine**; **Austin, Texas**; **Boise, Idaho**; **Columbus, Ohio**; **Des Moines, Iowa**; **Helena, Montana**; **Juneau, Alaska**; **Phoenix, Arizona**; and **Salem, Oregon**. **Mississippi** and **Alabama** presented problems for me. On their own, they don't have enough letters to generate enough words for a lesson. If you combine them with their capitals, they have too many letters. These states are represented by their capitals, **Jackson** and **Montgomery**.

The same procedure was used for important countries with short names. Italy is represented in two lessons—**Rome, Italy**, and **Venice, Italy. Paris, France**, assures representation for the French! Most of the Canadian provinces are represented, as are all of the Great Lakes and the seven continents.

Some common places have very short names. These cannot be secret places because they don't yield enough other words, but they can be words in the lessons. At the back of the book, you will find an index listing which lessons contain which places so that you can pick lessons that include places important to your class.

In choosing the words for each lesson, I have tried to include only words that most students would have in their listening/meaning vocabularies, but children vary in their word familiarity. If a word that is totally unknown to your class occurs in one of the lessons, you might want to omit that word from the lesson. Also, if there are words that you feel are inappropriate for your students, you may leave them out.

All of the *Making Places* lessons are multilevel. Multilevel means that there are a variety of things to learn and that each student can learn something from the lessons—although they probably all won't learn the same things. Just as in all Making Words lessons, each *Making Places* lesson contains some warm-up words (easy words, but NEVER use the word "easy" with your students!) and some harder words. Don't hesitate to do a lesson because most of your students won't be able to figure out the secret place! The secret place (and a few other tricky words) is there to challenge your top students. As long as all of your students are successfully making some of the words, then the lesson is a multilevel lesson from which each student is learning what he can learn at this point in time.

The sort step of the lesson is designed to draw students' attention to patterns. Every lesson contains sets of rhyming words that can be sorted by their rhyming patterns. Most lessons also contain some related words—words that share a common root and meaning. These two kinds of patterns—rhyming patterns and morphemic patterns—are the major tools for decoding and spelling as children progress through the grades. The lessons are multilevel in that both kinds of important patterns are dealt with in almost every lesson. (Some secret phrases just don't yield any related words, and thus the sorts in those lessons are only for the rhyming patterns.)

Recognizing rhyming and morphemic patterns is useless to your students if they don't use these skills to decode and spell words. Every lesson ends with a transfer step in which students decode and spell some new words based on the rhyming patterns in the words they made. To "bump up" the lesson a little, most of the transfer words have more than one syllable. Give students as much help as they need spelling the beginning (non-rhyming) parts of the words.

These learning opportunities just described are available in any Making Words lesson. However, *Making Places* lessons offer several additional learning opportunities:

- Students learn some geography by locating places on the map and talking about them.

- Students learn the meaning of some general geography terms (**continent**, **nation**, **capital**, etc.).

- Students learn some state and country capitals.

- Students learn that specific (proper) nouns require capital letters, but general (common) nouns do not.

- Students learn that you separate cities from states or countries with a comma.

It is fun to plan *Making Places* lessons. You may want to plan lessons for names of places in your community that are not included in this book. Simply go to *www.wordplays.com*, click on "Words in a Word," and type in the place name you want to use. Instantly, the computer will display all of the words (excluding some proper names) that you could use to plan a lesson customized for your class. I hope that you and the students will enjoy *Making Places* and that they will become more "geography savvy" as they gain decoding and spelling knowledge that will enable them all to be avid and successful readers and writers!

Afghanistan

a a a i f g h n n s t

Make Words: Tell children how many letters to use to make each word. (A slash in the Make Words list indicates that words can be made with the same letters. An underline __ in the letter bank or on the letter strip indicates that a blank space is needed for the secret place.)

Emphasize how changing just one letter or rearranging letters makes different words:

"Change 1 letter in **sight** to spell **fight**."

"Use the same letters in **thing** to spell **night**."

When children are not just adding or changing one letter, cue them to start over.

"Start over and use 5 new letters to spell **gifts**."

Give meaning or sentence clues when needed to clarify the word they are making:

"Start over and use 6 letters to spell **infant**. My brother is bigger than me now, but I remember when he was just a tiny **infant**."

Give children one minute to figure out the secret place and then give clues if needed.

"Our secret place is a country that begins with **A**."

Sort Rhymes

Reading Transfer: "Pretend you are reading and come to a new word." Have children put the words under the appropriate rhymes and use the rhymes to decode them.

Spelling Transfer: "Pretend you are writing and need to spell these words." Have children tell you how the words begin. Then, have children find and use the appropriate rhymes to finish spelling the new words.

Step-by-step directions for a sample *Making Places* lesson are on pages 9–13.

MAKE WORDS

gain
Asia
sing
sting
thing/night
sight
fight
gifts
giant
infant
against
Afghanistan

SORT WORDS

Rhymes:
night   sing
fight   thing
sight   sting

TRANSFER WORDS

Reading:
delight   earring

Spelling:
sunlight   string

Albany, New York

a a e o b k l n n r w y y , _ _

MAKE WORDS

own
near
year
wake
bake
baker
owner
Korea
Korean
yearly
bakery
Albany
Norway
Lebanon
Albany, New York

SORT WORDS

Related Words:
own, owner; Korea, Korean;
year, yearly;
bake, baker, bakery

Rhymes:
near   wake
year   bake

TRANSFER WORDS

Reading:
earthquake   appear

Spelling:
snowflake   disappear

Make Words: Tell children how many letters to use to make each word. (A slash in the Make Words list indicates that words can be made with the same letters. An underline __ in the letter bank or on the letter strip indicates that a blank space is needed for the secret place.)

Emphasize how changing just one letter or rearranging letters makes different words:

"Add a letter to **bake** to spell **baker**."

"Change 1 letter in **wake** to spell **bake**."

When children are not just adding or changing one letter, cue them to start over.

"Start over and use 5 new letters to spell **owner**."

Give meaning or sentence clues when needed to clarify the word they are making:

"Use 6 letters to spell **yearly**. I always look forward to our **yearly** family picnic."

Always alert children when they are making a name and expect them to use a capital letter.

"Take 7 letters and spell the country of **Lebanon**."

Give children one minute to figure out the secret place and then give clues if needed.

"Our secret place is a state and its capital, and you made the capital."

Sort Related Words

Sort Rhymes

Reading Transfer: "Pretend you are reading and come to a new word." Have children put the words under the appropriate rhymes and use the rhymes to decode them.

Spelling Transfer: "Pretend you are writing and need to spell these words." Have children tell you how the words begin. Then, have children find and use the appropriate rhymes to finish spelling the new words.

Step-by-step directions for a sample *Making Places* lesson are on pages 9–13.

Alberta

a a e b l r t

Make Words: Tell children how many letters to use to make each word. (A slash in the Make Words list indicates that words can be made with the same letters. An underline __ in the letter bank or on the letter strip indicates that a blank space is needed for the secret place.)

Emphasize how changing just one letter or rearranging letters makes different words:

> "Add a letter to **ate** to spell **late**."

> "Change 1 letter in **real** to spell **teal**."

> "Use the same letters in **eat** to spell **ate**."

When children are not just adding or changing one letter, cue them to start over.

> "Start over and use 5 new letters to spell **later**."

Give meaning or sentence clues when needed to clarify the word they are making:

> "Use the same letters in **table** to spell **bleat**. We could hear the goats **bleat**."

Always alert children when they are making a name and expect them to use a capital letter.

> "Take 6 letters and spell the name **Albert**."

Give children one minute to figure out the secret place and then give clues if needed.

> "Our secret place is a province in Canada that begins with an **A**."

Sort Related Words

Sort Rhymes

Reading Transfer: "Pretend you are reading and come to a new word." Have children put the words under the appropriate rhymes and use the rhymes to decode them.

Spelling Transfer: "Pretend you are writing and need to spell these words." Have children tell you how the words begin. Then, have children find and use the appropriate rhymes to finish spelling the new words.

Step-by-step directions for a sample *Making Places* lesson are on pages 9–13.

MAKE WORDS

eat/ate
late
real
teal
beat
able
table/bleat
later
Albert
Alberta

SORT WORDS

Related Words:
late, later

Rhymes:
| ate | eat | able |
| late | bleat | table |

TRANSFER WORDS

Reading:
tailgate   unstable

Spelling:
defeat   vibrate

Albuquerque

MAKE WORDS

rub
bar
bear/bare
bale/able
blue
real
rule
blare
equal
Albuquerque

SORT WORDS

Homophones:
bear, bare

Rhymes:
bare
blare

TRANSFER WORDS

Reading:
prepare   Delaware

Spelling:
compare   nightmare

Make Words: Tell children how many letters to use to make each word. (A slash in the Make Words list indicates that words can be made with the same letters. An underline __ in the letter bank or on the letter strip indicates that a blank space is needed for the secret place.)

Emphasize how changing just one letter or rearranging letters makes different words:

> "Add a letter to **bar** to spell **bear**. The **bear** slept all through the winter."

> "Use the same letters to spell another word that sounds exactly like **bear** but is spelled differently. When the trees lose their leaves, we say they are **bare**."

> "Use the same letters in **bale** to spell **able**."

When children are not just adding or changing one letter, cue them to start over.

> "Start over and use 5 new letters to spell **equal**."

Give meaning or sentence clues when needed to clarify the word they are making:

> "Start over and use 5 letters to spell **blare**. We could hear the **blare** of horns as the parade went down the street."

Give children one minute to figure out the secret place and then give clues if needed.

> "Our secret place is a city in New Mexico."

Sort Homophones

Sort Rhymes

Reading Transfer: "Pretend you are reading and come to a new word." Have children put the words under the appropriate rhymes and use the rhymes to decode them.

Spelling Transfer: "Pretend you are writing and need to spell these words." Have children tell you how the words begin. Then, have children find and use the appropriate rhymes to finish spelling the new words.

Step-by-step directions for a sample *Making Places* lesson are on pages 9–13.

Antarctica

a a a i c c n r t t

Make Words: Tell children how many letters to use to make each word. (A slash in the Make Words list indicates that words can be made with the same letters. An underline __ in the letter bank or on the letter strip indicates that a blank space is needed for the secret place.)

Emphasize how changing just one letter or rearranging letters makes different words:

"Add a letter to **rain** to spell **train**."

"Change 1 letter in **tart** to spell **cart**."

"Use the same letters in **act** to spell **cat**."

When children are not just adding or changing one letter, cue them to start over.

"Start over and use 4 new letters to spell **rant**."

Give meaning or sentence clues when needed to clarify the word they are making:

"Start over and use 6 letters to spell **Arctic**. The **Arctic** Ocean surrounds the North Pole and the **Arctic** Circle."

Give children one minute to figure out the secret place and then give clues if needed.

"Our secret place is a continent that begins with **A**."

Sort Related Words

Sort Rhymes

Reading Transfer: "Pretend you are reading and come to a new word." Have children put the words under the appropriate rhymes and use the rhymes to decode them.

Spelling Transfer: "Pretend you are writing and need to spell these words." Have children tell you how the words begin. Then, have children find and use the appropriate rhymes to finish spelling the new words.

Step-by-step directions for a sample *Making Places* lesson are on pages 9–13.

MAKE WORDS

ant
art
act/cat
car
tar
tart
cart
Iran
rant
rain
train
Arctic
Antarctica

SORT WORDS

Related Words:
Arctic, Antarctica

Rhymes:

ant	art	car	rain
rant	tart	tar	train
	cart		

TRANSFER WORDS

Reading:
transplant   guitar

Spelling:
contain   explain

Arctic Ocean

a a e i o c c c n r t __

MAKE WORDS

act
ace
ice
nice
rice
race
ocean/canoe
arena
react
action
concert
Croatia
reaction
Arctic Ocean

SORT WORDS

Related Words:
act, react, action, reaction

Rhymes:
ice   ace
nice   race
rice

TRANSFER WORDS

Reading:
sacrifice   replace

Spelling:
advice   fireplace

Make Words: Tell children how many letters to use to make each word. (A slash in the Make Words list indicates that words can be made with the same letters. An underline __ in the letter bank or on the letter strip indicates that a blank space is needed for the secret place.)

Emphasize how changing just one letter or rearranging letters makes different words:

"Add a letter to **ice** to spell **nice**."

"Change 1 letter in **nice** to spell **rice**."

"Use the same letters in **ocean** to spell **canoe**."

When children are not just adding or changing one letter, cue them to start over.

"Start over and use 5 new letters to spell **ocean**."

Give meaning or sentence clues when needed to clarify the word they are making:

"Start over and use 8 letters to spell **reaction**. Everyone waited to see her **reaction** to the news that she had won the contest."

Always alert children when they are making a name and expect them to use a capital letter.

"Take 7 letters and spell the country of **Croatia**. **Croatia** is a country in eastern Europe."

Give children one minute to figure out the secret place and then give clues if needed.

"Our secret place is an ocean with two words in its name."

Sort Related Words

Sort Rhymes

Reading Transfer: "Pretend you are reading and come to a new word." Have children put the words under the appropriate rhymes and use the rhymes to decode them.

Spelling Transfer: "Pretend you are writing and need to spell these words." Have children tell you how the words begin. Then, have children find and use the appropriate rhymes to finish spelling the new words.

Step-by-step directions for a sample *Making Places* lesson are on pages 9–13.

Argentina

Make Words: Tell children how many letters to use to make each word. (A slash in the Make Words list indicates that words can be made with the same letters. An underline __ in the letter bank or on the letter strip indicates that a blank space is needed for the secret place.)

Emphasize how changing just one letter or rearranging letters makes different words:

"Add 1 letter to **in** to spell **tin**."

"Change 1 letter in **gate** to spell **rate**."

"Use the same letters in **anger** to spell **range**."

When children are not just adding or changing one letter, cue them to start over.

"Start over and use 5 new letters to spell **grant**."

Give meaning or sentence clues when needed to clarify the word they are making:

"Use 7 letters to spell **granite**. The statue of the explorers was carved from **granite**."

Always alert children when they are making a name and expect them to use a capital letter.

"Add 1 letter to spell the name **Tina**."

Give children one minute to figure out the secret place and then give clues if needed.

"Our secret place is the name of a country in South America that starts with **A**."

Sort Related Words

Sort Rhymes

Reading Transfer: "Pretend you are reading and come to a new word." Have children put the words under the appropriate rhymes and use the rhymes to decode them.

Spelling Transfer: "Pretend you are writing and need to spell these words." Have children tell you how the words begin. Then, have children find and use the appropriate rhymes to finish spelling the new words.

Step-by-step directions for a sample *Making Places* lesson are on pages 9–13.

MAKE WORDS

in
tin
Tina
gate
rate
anger/range
grant
arena
inner
rating
granite
Argentina

SORT WORDS

Related Words:
rate, rating; in, inner

Rhymes:
gate   in
rate   tin

TRANSFER WORDS

Reading:
inflate   generate

Spelling:
debate   candidate

Arkansas

a a a k n r s s

MAKE WORDS

an
as
ask
ark
ran
rank
sank
Kara
Ankara
Kansas
Arkansas

SORT WORDS

Rhymes:
an   rank
ran   sank

TRANSFER WORDS

Reading:
outrank   caravan

Spelling:
suntan   began

Make Words: Tell children how many letters to use to make each word. (A slash in the Make Words list indicates that words can be made with the same letters. An underline __ in the letter bank or on the letter strip indicates that a blank space is needed for the secret place.)

Emphasize how changing just one letter or rearranging letters makes different words:

> "Add a letter to **ran** to spell **rank**."

> "Change 1 letter in **rank** to spell **sank**."

When children are not just adding or changing one letter, cue them to start over.

> "Start over and use 6 new letters to spell the state of **Kansas**."

Give meaning or sentence clues when needed to clarify the word they are making:

> "Start over and use 6 letters to spell **Ankara**. **Ankara** is the capital of Turkey."

Always alert children when they are making a name and expect them to use a capital letter.

> "Take 4 letters and spell the name **Kara**."

Give children one minute to figure out the secret place and then give clues if needed.

> "Our secret place is the name of a state that starts with **A**."

Sort Rhymes

Reading Transfer: "Pretend you are reading and come to a new word." Have children put the words under the appropriate rhymes and use the rhymes to decode them.

Spelling Transfer: "Pretend you are writing and need to spell these words." Have children tell you how the words begin. Then, have children find and use the appropriate rhymes to finish spelling the new words.

Step-by-step directions for a sample *Making Places* lesson are on pages 9–13.

Athens, Greece

a e e e e c g h n r s t , __

Make Words: Tell children how many letters to use to make each word. (A slash in the Make Words list indicates that words can be made with the same letters. An underline __ in the letter bank or on the letter strip indicates that a blank space is needed for the secret place.)

Emphasize how changing just one letter or rearranging letters makes different words:

"Add a letter to **heat** to spell **cheat**."

"Use the same letters in **teacher** to spell **cheater**."

When children are not just adding or changing one letter, cue them to start over.

"Start over and use 6 new letters to spell **grease**."

Give meaning or sentence clues when needed to clarify the word they are making:

"Use 6 letters to spell the country of **Greece**. **Greece** is a country in the Mediterranean."

Give children one minute to figure out the secret place and then give clues if needed.

"Our secret place is a country and its capital, and we spelled the country."

Sort Related Words

Sort Rhymes

Reading Transfer: "Pretend you are reading and come to a new word." Have children put the words under the appropriate rhymes and use the rhymes to decode them.

Spelling Transfer: "Pretend you are writing and need to spell these words." Have children tell you how the words begin. Then, have children find and use the appropriate rhymes to finish spelling the new words.

Step-by-step directions for a sample *Making Places* lesson are on pages 9–13.

MAKE WORDS

eat
each
heat
cheat/teach
range
grease
Greece
teacher/cheater
strange
teenager/generate
Athens, Greece

SORT WORDS

Related Words:
cheat, cheater; teach, teacher

Rhymes:

eat	each	range
heat	teach	strange
cheat		

TRANSFER WORDS

Reading:
arrange   retreat

Spelling:
exchange   impeach

Atlantic Ocean

MAKE WORDS

cone
tone
lone
line
nine
alone
ocean
inlet
nation
Latino
Laotian
Atlanta
national
Atlantic Ocean

SORT WORDS

Related Words:
nation, national; lone, alone

Rhymes:
cone   line
tone   nine
lone

TRANSFER WORDS

Reading:
headphone   sunshine

Spelling:
ozone   outline

Make Words: Tell children how many letters to use to make each word. (A slash in the Make Words list indicates that words can be made with the same letters. An underline __ in the letter bank or on the letter strip indicates that a blank space is needed for the secret place.)

Emphasize how changing just one letter or rearranging letters makes different words:

"Change 1 letter in **lone** to spell **line**."

When children are not just adding or changing one letter, cue them to start over.

"Start over and use 5 new letters to spell **alone**."

Give meaning or sentence clues when needed to clarify the word they are making:

"Start over and use 8 letters to spell **national**. The governors gathered in Washington for their **national** conference."

Always alert children when they are making a name and expect them to use a capital letter.

"Take 7 letters and spell **Laotian**. The **Laotian** family moved here from Laos."

Give children one minute to figure out the secret place and then give clues if needed.

"Our secret place is an ocean with two words in its name."

Sort Related Words

Sort Rhymes

Reading Transfer: "Pretend you are reading and come to a new word." Have children put the words under the appropriate rhymes and use the rhymes to decode them.

Spelling Transfer: "Pretend you are writing and need to spell these words." Have children tell you how the words begin. Then, have children find and use the appropriate rhymes to finish spelling the new words.

Step-by-step directions for a sample *Making Places* lesson are on pages 9–13.

Augusta, Maine

a a a e i u u g m n s t , __

Make Words: Tell children how many letters to use to make each word. (A slash in the Make Words list indicates that words can be made with the same letters. An underline __ in the letter bank or on the letter strip indicates that a blank space is needed for the secret place.)

Emphasize how changing just one letter or rearranging letters makes different words:

> "Change 1 letter in **gain** to spell **main**."

When children are not just adding or changing one letter, cue them to start over.

> "Start over and use 5 new letters to spell **amuse**."

Always alert children when they are making a name and expect them to use a capital letter.

> "Add 1 letter to spell the state of **Maine**."

Give meaning or sentence clues when needed to clarify the word they are making:

> "Start over and use 7 new letters to spell **animate**. The artist's job was to **animate** characters in *Snow White*."

Give children one minute to figure out the secret place and then give clues if needed.

> "Our secret place is a capital and its state, and we already spelled the state."

Sort Related Words

Sort Rhymes

Reading Transfer: "Pretend you are reading and come to a new word." Have children put the words under the appropriate rhymes and use the rhymes to decode them.

Spelling Transfer: "Pretend you are writing and need to spell these words." Have children tell you how the words begin. Then, have children find and use the appropriate rhymes to finish spelling the new words.

Step-by-step directions for a sample *Making Places* lesson are on pages 9–13.

MAKE WORDS

use
tie
gain
main
Maine
amuse
using
untie
August
amusing
animate
minutes
Augusta, Maine

SORT WORDS

Related Words:
use, using; amuse, amusing; tie, untie

Rhymes:
use   gain
amuse   main

TRANSFER WORDS

Reading:
accuse   obtain

Spelling:
sustain   refuse

Austin, Texas

a a e i u n s s t t x , __

MAKE WORDS

set
net
neat
seat
Asia
exit
taxi
taxes/Texas
sunset
tastes/states
status
statues
Austin, Texas

SORT WORDS

Related Words:
set, sunset

Rhymes:

set	neat
net	seat

TRANSFER WORDS

Reading:
quartet   mistreat

Spelling:
defeat   repeat

Make Words: Tell children how many letters to use to make each word. (A slash in the Make Words list indicates that words can be made with the same letters. An underline __ in the letter bank or on the letter strip indicates that a blank space is needed for the secret place.)

Emphasize how changing just one letter or rearranging letters makes different words:

"Add a letter to **status** to spell **statues**."

"Change 1 letter in **neat** to spell **seat**."

"Use the same letters in **tastes** to spell **states**."

When children are not just adding or changing one letter, cue them to start over.

"Start over and use 6 new letters to spell **sunset**."

Give meaning or sentence clues when needed to clarify the word they are making:

"Change 1 letter to spell **status**. When Jack called to check the **status** of his order, he was told that his package had already shipped."

Always alert children when they are making a name and expect them to use a capital letter.

"Use the same letters and spell the state of **Texas**."

Give children one minute to figure out the secret place and then give clues if needed.

"Our secret place is a capital and a state, and we spelled the state."

Sort Related Words

Sort Rhymes

Reading Transfer: "Pretend you are reading and come to a new word." Have children put the words under the appropriate rhymes and use the rhymes to decode them.

Spelling Transfer: "Pretend you are writing and need to spell these words." Have children tell you how the words begin. Then, have children find and use the appropriate rhymes to finish spelling the new words.

Step-by-step directions for a sample *Making Places* lesson are on pages 9–13.

Australia

a a a i u l r s t

Make Words: Tell children how many letters to use to make each word. (A slash in the Make Words list indicates that words can be made with the same letters. An underline __ in the letter bank or on the letter strip indicates that a blank space is needed for the secret place.)

Emphasize how changing just one letter or rearranging letters makes different words:

> "Add a letter to **sir** to spell **stir**."

> "Change 1 letter in **list** to spell **last**."

> "Use the same letters in **last** to spell **salt**."

When children are not just adding or changing one letter, cue them to start over.

> "Start over and use 4 new letters to spell the continent of **Asia**."

Give meaning or sentence clues when needed to clarify the word they are making:

> "Start over and use 5 letters to spell **Tulsa**. **Tulsa** is a large city in Oklahoma."

Always alert children when they are making a name and expect them to use a capital letter.

> "Take 7 letters and spell the country of **Austria**."

Give children one minute to figure out the secret place and then give clues if needed.

> "Our secret place is both a country and a continent."

Sort Rhymes

Reading Transfer: "Pretend you are reading and come to a new word." Have children put the words under the appropriate rhymes and use the rhymes to decode them.

Spelling Transfer: "Pretend you are writing and need to spell these words." Have children tell you how the words begin. Then, have children find and use the appropriate rhymes to finish spelling the new words.

Step-by-step directions for a sample *Making Places* lesson are on pages 9–13.

MAKE WORDS

air
art
sir
stir
list
last/salt
Asia
tail
trail/trial
atlas
Tulsa
Austria
Australia

SORT WORDS

Rhymes:
sir   tail
stir   trail

TRANSFER WORDS

Reading:
blackmail   prevail

Spelling:
retail   toenail

Baltimore

MAKE WORDS

oil
rim
Tim
time
lime
Rome
melt
belt
boil
able
table
broil
marble/ramble
Baltimore

SORT WORDS

Rhymes:
rim   oil   time   melt able
Tim   boil   lime   belt table
        broil

TRANSFER WORDS

Reading:
cable   turmoil

Spelling:
recoil   fable

Make Words: Tell children how many letters to use to make each word. (A slash in the Make Words list indicates that words can be made with the same letters. An underline __ in the letter bank or on the letter strip indicates that a blank space is needed for the secret place.)

Emphasize how changing just one letter or rearranging letters makes different words:

"Add a letter to **Tim** to spell **time**."

"Change 1 letter in **melt** to spell **belt**."

"Use the same letters in **marble** to spell **ramble**."

When children are not just adding or changing one letter, cue them to start over.

"Start over and use 5 new letters to spell **broil**."

Give meaning or sentence clues when needed to clarify the word they are making:

"Use the same 6 letters to spell **ramble**. We were not in a hurry so we decided to **ramble** through the park."

Always alert children when they are making a name and expect them to use a capital letter.

"Change 1 letter and spell the name **Tim**."

Give children one minute to figure out the secret place and then give clues if needed.

"Our secret place is the name of a city in Maryland."

Sort Rhymes

Reading Transfer: "Pretend you are reading and come to a new word." Have children put the words under the appropriate rhymes and use the rhymes to decode them.

Spelling Transfer: "Pretend you are writing and need to spell these words." Have children tell you how the words begin. Then, have children find and use the appropriate rhymes to finish spelling the new words.

Step-by-step directions for a sample *Making Places* lesson are on pages 9–13.

Baton Rouge

a e o o u b g n r t __

Make Words: Tell children how many letters to use to make each word. (A slash in the Make Words list indicates that words can be made with the same letters. An underline __ in the letter bank or on the letter strip indicates that a blank space is needed for the secret place.)

Emphasize how changing just one letter or rearranging letters makes different words:

> "Add a letter to **urban** to spell **turban**."

> "Change 1 letter in **beat** to spell **neat**."

When children are not just adding or changing one letter, cue them to start over.

> "Start over and use 6 new letters to spell **outran**."

Give meaning or sentence clues when needed to clarify the word they are making:

> "Start over and use 6 letters to spell **urgent**. The television program was interrupted with an **urgent** warning about an approaching tornado."

Always alert children when they are making a name and expect them to use a capital letter.

> "Take 4 letters and spell the city of **Reno**."

Give children one minute to figure out the secret place and then give clues if needed.

> "Our secret place is the capital of Louisiana."

Sort Related Words

Sort Rhymes

Reading Transfer: "Pretend you are reading and come to a new word." Have children put the words under the appropriate rhymes and use the rhymes to decode them.

Spelling Transfer: "Pretend you are writing and need to spell these words." Have children tell you how the words begin. Then, have children find and use the appropriate rhymes to finish spelling the new words.

Step-by-step directions for a sample *Making Places* lesson are on pages 9–13.

MAKE WORDS

ran
age
rage
beat
neat
Reno
agent
urban
turban
urgent
outran
outrage
Baton Rouge

SORT WORDS

Related Words:
ran, outran; rage, outrage

Rhymes:

age	beat	urban
rage	neat	turban

TRANSFER WORDS

Reading:
defeat   birdcage

Spelling:
engage   repeat

Beijing, China

MAKE WORDS

ice
nice
each
beach
icing
niche
cabin
chain/China
change
Beijing, China

SORT WORDS

Related Words:
ice, icing

Rhymes:
ice   each
nice   beach

TRANSFER WORDS

Reading:
device   outreach

Spelling:
advice   impeach

Make Words: Tell children how many letters to use to make each word. (A slash in the Make Words list indicates that words can be made with the same letters. An underline __ in the letter bank or on the letter strip indicates that a blank space is needed for the secret place.)

Emphasize how changing just one letter or rearranging letters makes different words:

"Add a letter to **ice** to spell **nice**."

"Use the same letters in **chain** to spell the country of **China**."

When children are not just adding or changing one letter, cue them to start over.

"Start over and use 5 new letters to spell **cabin**."

Give meaning or sentence clues when needed to clarify the word they are making:

"Start over and use 5 letters to spell **niche**. After trying several jobs, the woman found her **niche** as a personal chef."

Give children one minute to figure out the secret place and then give clues if needed.

"Our secret place is a capital and a country, and we made the name of the country."

Sort Related Words

Sort Rhymes

Reading Transfer: "Pretend you are reading and come to a new word." Have children put the words under the appropriate rhymes and use the rhymes to decode them.

Spelling Transfer: "Pretend you are writing and need to spell these words." Have children tell you how the words begin. Then, have children find and use the appropriate rhymes to finish spelling the new words.

Step-by-step directions for a sample *Making Places* lesson are on pages 9–13.

Birmingham

a i i b g h m m n r

Make Words: Tell children how many letters to use to make each word. (A slash in the Make Words list indicates that words can be made with the same letters. An underline __ in the letter bank or on the letter strip indicates that a blank space is needed for the secret place.)

Emphasize how changing just one letter or rearranging letters makes different words:

"Add a letter to **gain** to spell **grain**."

"Change 1 letter in **grain** to spell **brain**."

"Use the same letters in **margin** to spell **arming**."

When children are not just adding or changing one letter, cue them to start over.

"Start over and use 4 new letters to spell the country of **Iran**."

Give meaning or sentence clues when needed to clarify the word they are making:

"Use 6 letters to spell **margin**. Set the computer for the size of your left **margin**."

Always alert children when they are making a name and expect them to use a capital letter.

"Take 5 letters and spell the city of **Miami**."

Give children one minute to figure out the secret place and then give clues if needed.

"Our secret place is the name of a city in Alabama that begins with **B**."

Sort Related Words

Sort Rhymes

Reading Transfer: "Pretend you are reading and come to a new word." Have children put the words under the appropriate rhymes and use the rhymes to decode them.

Spelling Transfer: "Pretend you are writing and need to spell these words." Have children tell you how the words begin. Then, have children find and use the appropriate rhymes to finish spelling the new words.

Step-by-step directions for a sample *Making Places* lesson are on pages 9–13.

MAKE WORDS

air
arm
harm
hair
Iran/rain
gain
grain
brain
Miami
margin/arming
harming
Birmingham

SORT WORDS

Related Words:
arm, arming; harm, harming

Rhymes:

arm	arming	rain	air
harm	harming	grain	hair
		gain	
		brain	

TRANSFER WORDS

Reading:
despair   disarm

Spelling:
complain   repair

Boise, Idaho

a e i i o o b d h s , ＿

MAKE WORDS

bed
shed
hide
side
idea
soda
bias
shade
beads
Idaho
bodies
Boise, Idaho

SORT WORDS

Rhymes:
bed   hide
shed   side

TRANSFER WORDS

Reading:
purebred   collide

Spelling:
decide   confide

Make Words: Tell children how many letters to use to make each word. (A slash in the Make Words list indicates that words can be made with the same letters. An underline ＿ in the letter bank or on the letter strip indicates that a blank space is needed for the secret place.)

Emphasize how changing just one letter or rearranging letters makes different words:

"Change 1 letter in **hide** to spell **side**."

When children are not just adding or changing one letter, cue them to start over.

"Start over and use 5 new letters to spell **shade**."

Give meaning or sentence clues when needed to clarify the word they are making:

"Start over and use 4 new letters to spell **bias**. A good teacher has no **bias** against boys or girls."

Give children one minute to figure out the secret place and then give clues if needed.

"Our secret place is a capital and its state, and we already spelled the state."

Sort Rhymes

Reading Transfer: "Pretend you are reading and come to a new word." Have children put the words under the appropriate rhymes and use the rhymes to decode them.

Spelling Transfer: "Pretend you are writing and need to spell these words." Have children tell you how the words begin. Then, have children find and use the appropriate rhymes to finish spelling the new words.

Step-by-step directions for a sample *Making Places* lesson are on pages 9–13.

Boston

o o b n s t

Make Words: Tell children how many letters to use to make each word. (A slash in the Make Words list indicates that words can be made with the same letters. An underline __ in the letter bank or on the letter strip indicates that a blank space is needed for the secret place.)

Emphasize how changing just one letter or rearranging letters makes different words:

"Change 1 letter in **boon** to spell **boot**."

"Use the same letters in **boots** to spell **boost**."

When children are not just adding or changing one letter, cue them to start over.

"Start over and use 4 letters to spell **snob**."

Give meaning or sentence clues when needed to clarify the word they are making:

"Add a letter to **boo** to spell **boon**. When the car factory located in our town, it was a **boon** to the whole economy."

Give children one minute to figure out the secret place and then give clues if needed.

"Our secret place is the capital of Massachusetts and begins with **B**."

Sort Related Words

Sort Rhymes

Reading Transfer: "Pretend you are reading and come to a new word." Have children put the words under the appropriate rhymes and use the rhymes to decode them.

Spelling Transfer: "Pretend you are writing and need to spell these words." Have children tell you how the words begin. Then, have children find and use the appropriate rhymes to finish spelling the new words.

Step-by-step directions for a sample *Making Places* lesson are on pages 9–13.

MAKE WORDS

sob
son
ton
too
boo
boon
boot
soon
snob
boots/boost
Boston

SORT WORDS

Related Words:
boot, boots

Rhymes:

sob	too	boon	son
snob	boo	soon	ton

TRANSFER WORDS

Reading:
doorknob   balloon

Spelling:
shampoo   cartoon

British Columbia

MAKE WORDS

arm
harm
tour
Utah
charm
chart
smart
storm
tourism
abolish
British
historic
hailstorm
British Columbia

SORT WORDS

Related Words:
tour, tourism;
storm, hailstorm

Rhymes:
arm   chart
harm   smart
charm

TRANSFER WORDS

Reading:
disarm   depart

Spelling:
outsmart alarm

Make Words: Tell children how many letters to use to make each word. (A slash in the Make Words list indicates that words can be made with the same letters. An underline __ in the letter bank or on the letter strip indicates that a blank space is needed for the secret place.)

Emphasize how changing just one letter or rearranging letters makes different words:

> "Add a letter to **arm** to spell **harm**."

> "Change 1 letter in **charm** to spell **chart**."

When children are not just adding or changing one letter, cue them to start over.

> "Start over and use 7 new letters to spell **tourism**."

Give meaning or sentence clues when needed to clarify the word they are making:

> "Use 7 letters to spell **abolish**. Many students would like to **abolish** end-of-year testing."

Always alert children when they are making a name and expect them to use a capital letter.

> "Take 7 letters and spell **British**. **British** people are from Great Britain."

Give children one minute to figure out the secret place and then give clues if needed.

> "Our secret place is a province in Canada with two words, and we already spelled one of the words."

Sort Related Words

Sort Rhymes

Reading Transfer: "Pretend you are reading and come to a new word." Have children put the words under the appropriate rhymes and use the rhymes to decode them.

Spelling Transfer: "Pretend you are writing and need to spell these words." Have children tell you how the words begin. Then, have children find and use the appropriate rhymes to finish spelling the new words.

Step-by-step directions for a sample *Making Places* lesson are on pages 9–13.

Cairo, Egypt

a e i o c g p r t y , __

Make Words: Tell children how many letters to use to make each word. (A slash in the Make Words list indicates that words can be made with the same letters. An underline __ in the letter bank or on the letter strip indicates that a blank space is needed for the secret place.)

Emphasize how changing just one letter or rearranging letters makes different words:

"Add a letter to **age** to spell **page**."

"Change the last 2 letters in **poetry** to spell **poetic**."

When children are not just adding or changing one letter, cue them to start over.

"Start over and use 5 new letters to spell **opera**."

Give meaning or sentence clues when needed to clarify the word they are making:

"Start over and use 8 letters to spell **category**. The JEOPARDY!® winner did very well in the States and Capitals **category**."

Give children one minute to figure out the secret place and then give clues if needed.

"Our secret place is the name of a capital and country. The Great Pyramids are found in this country."

Sort Related Words

Sort Rhymes

Reading Transfer: "Pretend you are reading and come to a new word." Have children put the words under the appropriate rhymes and use the rhymes to decode them.

Spelling Transfer: "Pretend you are writing and need to spell these words." Have children tell you how the words begin. Then, have children find and use the appropriate rhymes to finish spelling the new words.

Step-by-step directions for a sample *Making Places* lesson are on pages 9–13.

MAKE WORDS

ice
age
page
yoga
poet
rice
price
opera
poetry
poetic
category
Cairo, Egypt

SORT WORDS

Related Words:
poet, poetry, poetic

Rhymes:
ice   age
rice   page
price

TRANSFER WORDS

Reading:
entice enrage

Spelling:
advice backstage

California

a a i i o c f l n r

MAKE WORDS

oil
coil
foil
fail
nail
rail
frail
canal
Carol/coral
oilcan
Africa
African
California

SORT WORDS

Related Words:
oil, oilcan; Africa, African

Rhymes:
fail   oil
nail   coil
rail   foil
frail

TRANSFER WORDS

Reading:
fingernail   turmoil

Spelling:
prevail   recoil

Make Words: Tell children how many letters to use to make each word. (A slash in the Make Words list indicates that words can be made with the same letters. An underline __ in the letter bank or on the letter strip indicates that a blank space is needed for the secret place.)

Emphasize how changing just one letter or rearranging letters makes different words:

"Add a letter to **oil** to spell **coil**."

"Change 1 letter in **foil** to spell **fail**."

"Use the same letters in **Carol** to spell **coral**."

When children are not just adding or changing one letter, cue them to start over.

"Start over and use 5 new letters to spell **canal**."

Give meaning or sentence clues when needed to clarify the word they are making:

"Start over and use 6 letters to spell **oilcan**. All of the oil spilled out of the **oilcan**."

Always alert children when they are making a name and expect them to use a capital letter.

"Take 6 letters and spell the continent of **Africa**."

Give children one minute to figure out the secret place and then give clues if needed.

"Our secret place is the name of a state that starts with **C**."

Sort Related Words

Sort Rhymes

Reading Transfer: "Pretend you are reading and come to a new word." Have children put the words under the appropriate rhymes and use the rhymes to decode them.

Spelling Transfer: "Pretend you are writing and need to spell these words." Have children tell you how the words begin. Then, have children find and use the appropriate rhymes to finish spelling the new words.

Step-by-step directions for a sample *Making Places* lesson are on pages 9–13.

capitals

a a i c l p s t

Make Words: Tell children how many letters to use to make each word. (A slash in the Make Words list indicates that words can be made with the same letters. An underline __ in the letter bank or on the letter strip indicates that a blank space is needed for the secret place.)

Emphasize how changing just one letter or rearranging letters makes different words:

> "Add a letter to **lip** to spell **slip**."

> "Change 1 letter in **slip** to spell **clip**."

When children are not just adding or changing one letter, cue them to start over.

> "Start over and use 4 new letters to spell **pail**."

Give meaning or sentence clues when needed to clarify the word they are making:

> "Start over and use 7 letters to spell **plastic**. The dish fell but didn't break because it was made of **plastic**."

Give children one minute to figure out the secret place and then give clues if needed.

> "Our secret place is not a specific place this time. It refers to many important cities and begins with a lowercase **c**."

Sort Rhymes

Reading Transfer: "Pretend you are reading and come to a new word." Have children put the words under the appropriate rhymes and use the rhymes to decode them.

Spelling Transfer: "Pretend you are writing and need to spell these words." Have children tell you how the words begin. Then, have children find and use the appropriate rhymes to finish spelling the new words.

Step-by-step directions for a sample *Making Places* lesson are on pages 9–13.

MAKE WORDS

cat
cap
lap
tap
tip
lip
slip
clip
pail
tail
plastic
capitals

SORT WORDS

Rhymes:

tip	cap	pail
lip	lap	tail
slip	tap	
clip		

TRANSFER WORDS

Reading:
friendship   hubcap

Spelling:
spaceship   unwrap

Charleston

a e o c h l n r s t

MAKE WORDS

ate/eat
heat/hate
Reno
latch
ocean
coast
roast
snatch
Athens
Charles
treason
ancestor
Charleston

SORT WORDS

Rhymes:

eat	ate	latch	coast
heat	hate	snatch	roast

TRANSFER WORDS

Reading:
dispatch   calculate
Spelling:
repeat   rematch

Make Words: Tell children how many letters to use to make each word. (A slash in the Make Words list indicates that words can be made with the same letters. An underline __ in the letter bank or on the letter strip indicates that a blank space is needed for the secret place.)

Emphasize how changing just one letter or rearranging letters makes different words:

> "Add a letter to **eat** to spell **heat**."

> "Change 1 letter in **coast** to spell **roast**."

> "Use the same letters in **heat** to spell **hate**."

When children are not just adding or changing one letter, cue them to start over.

> "Start over and use 6 new letters to spell **snatch**."

Give meaning or sentence clues when needed to clarify the word they are making:

> "Start over and use 7 letters to spell **treason**. The spy was convicted of **treason**."

Always alert children when they are making a name and expect them to use a capital letter.

> "Start over and use 6 new letters to spell the city of **Athens**. **Athens** is the capital of Greece."

Give children one minute to figure out the secret place and then give clues if needed.

> "Our secret place is a city in West Virginia and also a city in South Carolina. It begins with **Ch**."

Sort Rhymes

Reading Transfer: "Pretend you are reading and come to a new word." Have children put the words under the appropriate rhymes and use the rhymes to decode them.

Spelling Transfer: "Pretend you are writing and need to spell these words." Have children tell you how the words begin. Then, have children find and use the appropriate rhymes to finish spelling the new words.

Step-by-step directions for a sample *Making Places* lesson are on pages 9–13.

Charlotte

a e o c h l r t t

Make Words: Tell children how many letters to use to make each word. (A slash in the Make Words list indicates that words can be made with the same letters. An underline __ in the letter bank or on the letter strip indicates that a blank space is needed for the secret place.)

Emphasize how changing just one letter or rearranging letters makes different words:

> "Add a letter to **core** to spell **chore**."

> "Change a letter in **hot** to spell **cot**."

When children are not just adding or changing one letter, cue them to start over.

> "Start over and use 6 letters to spell **hotter**."

Give meaning or sentence clues when needed to clarify the word they are making:

> "Change 1 letter to spell **clatter**. There was a great **clatter** in the kitchen when the pots fell off the shelf."

Give children one minute to figure out the secret place and then give clues if needed.

> "Our secret place is the name of a city in North Carolina that begins with **Ch**."

Sort Related Words

Sort Rhymes

Reading Transfer: "Pretend you are reading and come to a new word." Have children put the words under the appropriate rhymes and use the rhymes to decode them.

Spelling Transfer: "Pretend you are writing and need to spell these words." Have children tell you how the words begin. Then, have children find and use the appropriate rhymes to finish spelling the new words.

Step-by-step directions for a sample *Making Places* lesson are on pages 9–13.

MAKE WORDS

hot
cot
coat
each
core
chore
reach
teach
throat
threat
hotter
chatter
clatter
Charlotte

SORT WORDS

Related Words:
hot, hotter

Rhymes:
chatter	coat	hot	core
clatter	throat	cot	chore

each
reach
teach

TRANSFER WORDS

Reading:
matter   flatter

Spelling:
platter   splatter

Cleveland

MAKE WORDS

all
ace
lace
call
even
lean
clean
dance
leave
level
candle
called
leaned
cleaned
Cleveland

SORT WORDS

Related Words:
lean, leaned; clean, cleaned;
call, called

Rhymes:

all	lean	leaned	ace
call	clean	cleaned	lace

TRANSFER WORDS

Reading:
install   embrace

Spelling:
replace   recall

Make Words: Tell children how many letters to use to make each word. (A slash in the Make Words list indicates that words can be made with the same letters. An underline __ in the letter bank or on the letter strip indicates that a blank space is needed for the secret place.)

Emphasize how changing just one letter or rearranging letters makes different words:

"Add a letter to **lean** to spell **clean**."

When children are not just adding or changing one letter, cue them to start over.

"Start over and use 6 new letters to spell **candle**."

Give meaning or sentence clues when needed to clarify the word they are making:

"Start over and use 5 letters to spell **level**. We used a **level** to hang the pictures straight."

Give children one minute to figure out the secret place and then give clues if needed.

"Our secret place is a city in Ohio that begins with **C**."

Sort Related Words

Sort Rhymes

Reading Transfer: "Pretend you are reading and come to a new word." Have children put the words under the appropriate rhymes and use the rhymes to decode them.

Spelling Transfer: "Pretend you are writing and need to spell these words." Have children tell you how the words begin. Then, have children find and use the appropriate rhymes to finish spelling the new words.

Step-by-step directions for a sample *Making Places* lesson are on pages 9–13.

Colombia

a i o o b c l m

Make Words: Tell children how many letters to use to make each word. (A slash in the Make Words list indicates that words can be made with the same letters. An underline __ in the letter bank or on the letter strip indicates that a blank space is needed for the secret place.)

Emphasize how changing just one letter or rearranging letters makes different words:

"Add a letter to **am** to spell **aim**."

"Change 1 letter in **coil** to spell **boil**."

When children are not just adding or changing one letter, cue them to start over.

"Start over and use 5 new letters to spell **bloom**."

Give meaning or sentence clues when needed to clarify the word they are making:

"Add a letter to spell **abloom**. Washington, D.C., was glorious with the cherry trees all **abloom**."

Always alert children when they are making a name and expect them to use a capital letter.

"Start over and use 4 new letters to spell the city of **Lima**. **Lima** is the capital of Peru."

Give children one minute to figure out the secret place and then give clues if needed.

"Our secret place is a country in South America that begins with **C**."

Sort Related Words

Sort Rhymes

Reading Transfer: "Pretend you are reading and come to a new word." Have children put the words under the appropriate rhymes and use the rhymes to decode them.

Spelling Transfer: "Pretend you are writing and need to spell these words." Have children tell you how the words begin. Then, have children find and use the appropriate rhymes to finish spelling the new words.

Step-by-step directions for a sample *Making Places* lesson are on pages 9–13.

MAKE WORDS

am
aim
oil
coil
boil
boom
Lima
clam
claim
bloom
abloom
Colombia

SORT WORDS

Related Words:
bloom, abloom

Rhymes:

aim	boom	am	oil
claim	bloom	clam	coil
	abloom		boil

TRANSFER WORDS

Reading:
courtroom   recoil

Spelling:
turmoil   exclaim

Colorado

MAKE WORDS

old
cold
cord
lord
load
road
door/odor
cool
drool
Carol/coral
color
Colorado

SORT WORDS

Rhymes:

old	load	cord	cool
cold	road	lord	drool

TRANSFER WORDS

Reading:
afford   whirlpool

Spelling:
record   preschool

Make Words: Tell children how many letters to use to make each word. (A slash in the Make Words list indicates that words can be made with the same letters. An underline __ in the letter bank or on the letter strip indicates that a blank space is needed for the secret place.)

Emphasize how changing just one letter or rearranging letters makes different words:

> "Add a letter to **old** to spell **cold**."

> "Change 1 letter in **cord** to spell **lord**."

> "Use the same letters in **door** to spell **odor**."

When children are not just adding or changing one letter, cue them to start over.

> "Start over and use 4 new letters to spell **door**."

Give meaning or sentence clues when needed to clarify the word they are making:

> "Use the same letters to spell **coral**. Jim and David snorkeled around the **coral** reef."

Always alert children when they are making a name and expect them to use a capital letter.

> "Start over and use 5 new letters to spell the name **Carol**."

Give children one minute to figure out the secret place and then give clues if needed.

> "Our secret place is the name of a state that starts with **C**."

Sort Rhymes

Reading Transfer: "Pretend you are reading and come to a new word." Have children put the words under the appropriate rhymes and use the rhymes to decode them.

Spelling Transfer: "Pretend you are writing and need to spell these words." Have children tell you how the words begin. Then, have children find and use the appropriate rhymes to finish spelling the new words.

Step-by-step directions for a sample *Making Places* lesson are on pages 9–13.

44

Columbus, Ohio

i o o o u u b c h l m s , ___

Make Words: Tell children how many letters to use to make each word. (A slash in the Make Words list indicates that words can be made with the same letters. An underline ___ in the letter bank or on the letter strip indicates that a blank space is needed for the secret place.)

Emphasize how changing just one letter or rearranging letters makes different words:

> "Add a letter to **oil** to spell **boil**."

> "Change 1 letter in **coil** to spell **cool**."

When children are not just adding or changing one letter, cue them to start over.

> "Start over and use 5 new letters to spell **music**."

Always alert children when they are making a name and expect them to use a capital letter.

> "Take 8 letters and spell **Columbus**. **Columbus** is the capital of a U.S. state."

Give meaning or sentence clues when needed to clarify the word they are making:

> "Start over and use 5 new letters to spell **combo**. He got the chicken **combo** special."

Give children one minute to figure out the secret place and then give clues if needed.

> "Our secret place is a capital and its state, and we already spelled the capital."

Sort Rhymes

Reading Transfer: "Pretend you are reading and come to a new word." Have children put the words under the appropriate rhymes and use the rhymes to decode them.

Spelling Transfer: "Pretend you are writing and need to spell these words." Have children tell you how the words begin. Then, have children find and use the appropriate rhymes to finish spelling the new words.

Step-by-step directions for a sample *Making Places* lesson are on pages 9–13.

MAKE WORDS

oil
boil
coil
cool
loom
boom
bloom
combo
music
school
Columbus
Columbus, Ohio

SORT WORDS

Rhymes:

oil	loom	cool
boil	boom	school
coil	bloom	

TRANSFER WORDS

Reading:
mushroom   whirlpool

Spelling:
turmoil   classroom

Connecticut

e i o u c c c n n t t

MAKE WORDS

cut
nut
tie
one
none
tent
cent
once
ounce
untie/unite
union
content
connect
Connecticut

SORT WORDS

Related Words:
tie, untie; one, once

Rhymes:
| tent | one | cut |
| cent | none | nut |

TRANSFER WORDS

Reading:
shortcut   percent

Spelling:
invent   prevent

Make Words: Tell children how many letters to use to make each word. (A slash in the Make Words list indicates that words can be made with the same letters. An underline __ in the letter bank or on the letter strip indicates that a blank space is needed for the secret place.)

Emphasize how changing just one letter or rearranging letters makes different words:

"Add a letter to **once** to spell **ounce**."

"Change 1 letter in **cut** to spell **nut**."

"Use the same letters in **untie** to spell **unite**."

When children are not just adding or changing one letter, cue them to start over.

"Start over and use 5 new letters to spell **untie**."

Give meaning or sentence clues when needed to clarify the word they are making:

"Change the last 2 letters to spell **union**. My mom belongs to the **union**."

Give children one minute to figure out the secret place and then give clues if needed.

"Our secret place is the name of a state that you can spell by adding your letters to **connect**."

Sort Related Words

Sort Rhymes

Reading Transfer: "Pretend you are reading and come to a new word." Have children put the words under the appropriate rhymes and use the rhymes to decode them.

Spelling Transfer: "Pretend you are writing and need to spell these words." Have children tell you how the words begin. Then, have children find and use the appropriate rhymes to finish spelling the new words.

Step-by-step directions for a sample *Making Places* lesson are on pages 9–13.

continents

e i o c n n n s t t

Make Words: Tell children how many letters to use to make each word. (A slash in the Make Words list indicates that words can be made with the same letters. An underline __ in the letter bank or on the letter strip indicates that a blank space is needed for the secret place.)

Emphasize how changing just one letter or rearranging letters makes different words:

> "Add a letter to **tone** to spell **stone**."

> "Change 1 letter in **contest** to spell **content**."

When children are not just adding or changing one letter, cue them to start over.

> "Start over and use 6 new letters to spell **tennis**."

Give meaning or sentence clues when needed to clarify the word they are making:

> "Change one letter to spell **cent**. One penny is worth one **cent**."

Give children one minute to figure out the secret place and then give clues if needed.

> "Our secret place is not a specific place this time. The word begins with a lowercase letter. There are seven of them, and Europe is one."

Sort Homophones

Sort Rhymes

Reading Transfer: "Pretend you are reading and come to a new word." Have children put the words under the appropriate rhymes and use the rhymes to decode them.

Spelling Transfer: "Pretend you are writing and need to spell these words." Have children tell you how the words begin. Then, have children find and use the appropriate rhymes to finish spelling the new words.

Step-by-step directions for a sample *Making Places* lesson are on pages 9–13.

MAKE WORDS

not
cot
coin
sent
cent
cone
tone
stone
tennis
contest
content
innocent
continents

SORT WORDS

Homophones:
sent, cent

Rhymes:
not   cone
cot   tone
         stone

TRANSFER WORDS

Reading:
trombone   jackpot

Spelling:
robot   postpone

countries

e i o u c n r s t

MAKE WORDS

tie
nest
rest
Reno
cone
tone
stone/notes
untie/unite
counties
countries

SORT WORDS

Related Words:
tie, untie

Rhymes:
nest   cone
rest   tone
        stone

TRANSFER WORDS

Reading:
saxophone   suggest

Spelling:
contest   backbone

Make Words: Tell children how many letters to use to make each word. (A slash in the Make Words list indicates that words can be made with the same letters. An underline __ in the letter bank or on the letter strip indicates that a blank space is needed for the secret place.)

Emphasize how changing just one letter or rearranging letters makes different words:

> "Add a letter to **tone** to spell **stone**."

> "Change a letter in **cone** to spell **tone**."

> "Use the same letters in **stone** to spell **notes**."

When children are not just adding or changing one letter, cue them to start over.

> "Start over and use 8 new letters to spell **counties**."

Give meaning or sentence clues when needed to clarify the word they are making:

> "Use the same 5 letters to spell **unite**. The whole state will **unite** to support the team that wins the state championship."

Always alert children when they are making a name and expect them to use a capital letter.

> "Start over and use 4 letters to spell the city of **Reno**. **Reno** is a large city in Nevada."

Give children one minute to figure out the secret place and then give clues if needed.

> "Our secret place is another word for nations that begins with a **c**."

Sort Related Words

Sort Rhymes

Reading Transfer: "Pretend you are reading and come to a new word." Have children put the words under the appropriate rhymes and use the rhymes to decode them.

Spelling Transfer: "Pretend you are writing and need to spell these words." Have children tell you how the words begin. Then, have children find and use the appropriate rhymes to finish spelling the new words.

Step-by-step directions for a sample *Making Places* lesson are on pages 9–13.

Delaware

a a e e d l r w

Make Words: Tell children how many letters to use to make each word. (A slash in the Make Words list indicates that words can be made with the same letters. An underline ___ in the letter bank or on the letter strip indicates that a blank space is needed for the secret place.)

Emphasize how changing just one letter or rearranging letters makes different words:

> "Add a letter to **dew** to spell **drew**."

> "Change 1 letter in **lead** to spell **read**."

> "Use the same letters in **deal** to spell **lead**."

When children are not just adding or changing one letter, cue them to start over.

> "Start over and use 6 new letters to spell **leader**."

Give meaning or sentence clues when needed to clarify the word they are making:

> "Change 1 letter to spell another kind of **deer**. We stopped and watched the **deer** cross the road."

Give children one minute to figure out the secret place and then give clues if needed.

> "Our secret place is the name of a state that starts with **D**."

Sort Homophones

Sort Related Words

Sort Rhymes

Reading Transfer: "Pretend you are reading and come to a new word." Have children put the words under the appropriate rhymes and use the rhymes to decode them.

Spelling Transfer: "Pretend you are writing and need to spell these words." Have children tell you how the words begin. Then, have children find and use the appropriate rhymes to finish spelling the new words.

Step-by-step directions for a sample *Making Places* lesson are on pages 9–13.

MAKE WORDS

law
raw
dew
drew
draw
real
deal/lead
read/dear
deer
leader/dealer
Delaware

SORT WORDS

Homophones:
deer, dear

Related Words:
draw, drew; lead, leader; deal, dealer

Rhymes:

law	dew	lead	real
raw	drew	read	deal
draw			

TRANSFER WORDS

Reading:
conceal   withdraw

Spelling:
withdrew   reveal

Denmark

a e d k m n r

MAKE WORDS

make
rake
rank
Dean
mean
dark
mark
Karen
darken
marked
ranked
Denmark

SORT WORDS

Related Words:
dark, darken; rank, ranked;
mark, marked

Rhymes:
dark   Dean   make
mark   mean   rake

TRANSFER WORDS

Reading:
remark   overtake

Spelling:
mistake   ballpark

Make Words: Tell children how many letters to use to make each word. (A slash in the Make Words list indicates that words can be made with the same letters. An underline __ in the letter bank or on the letter strip indicates that a blank space is needed for the secret place.)

Emphasize how changing just one letter or rearranging letters makes different words:

"Change 1 letter in **dark** to spell **mark**."

When children are not just adding or changing one letter, cue them to start over.

"Start over and use 6 new letters to spell **darken**."

Give meaning or sentence clues when needed to clarify the word they are making:

"Start over and use 6 letters to spell **ranked**. Our basketball team was **ranked** second in the state at the beginning of the season."

Always alert children when they are making a name and expect them to use a capital letter.

"Take 5 letters and spell the name **Karen**."

Give children one minute to figure out the secret place and then give clues if needed.

"Our secret place is a country that begins with **D**."

Sort Related Words

Sort Rhymes

Reading Transfer: "Pretend you are reading and come to a new word." Have children put the words under the appropriate rhymes and use the rhymes to decode them.

Spelling Transfer: "Pretend you are writing and need to spell these words." Have children tell you how the words begin. Then, have children find and use the appropriate rhymes to finish spelling the new words.

Step-by-step directions for a sample *Making Places* lesson are on pages 9–13.

Des Moines, Iowa

a e e i i o o d m n s s w , __ __

Make Words: Tell children how many letters to use to make each word. (A slash in the Make Words list indicates that words can be made with the same letters. An underline __ in the letter bank or on the letter strip indicates that a blank space is needed for the secret place.)

Emphasize how changing just one letter or rearranging letters makes different words:

> "Add 2 letters to **wood** to spell **wooden**."

> "Change 1 letter in **side** to spell **wide**."

When children are not just adding or changing one letter, cue them to start over.

> "Start over and use 7 new letters to spell **disease**."

Always alert children when they are making a name and expect them to use a capital letter.

> "Take 4 letters and spell the state of **Iowa**."

Give meaning or sentence clues when needed to clarify the word they are making:

> "Start over and use 7 new letters to spell **madness**. No one understood the reason for her **madness** and anger."

Give children one minute to figure out the secret place and then give clues if needed.

> "Our secret place is a capital and its state, and we already spelled the state."

Sort Related Words

Sort Rhymes

Reading Transfer: "Pretend you are reading and come to a new word." Have children put the words under the appropriate rhymes and use the rhymes to decode them.

Spelling Transfer: "Pretend you are writing and need to spell these words." Have children tell you how the words begin. Then, have children find and use the appropriate rhymes to finish spelling the new words.

Step-by-step directions for a sample *Making Places* lesson are on pages 9–13.

MAKE WORDS

mad
sad
Iowa
side
wide
seed
weed
wood
wooden
Sweden
madness
disease
mission
Des Moines, Iowa

SORT WORDS

Related Words:
mad, madness; wood, wooden

Rhymes:

seed	mad	side
weed	sad	wide

TRANSFER WORDS

Reading:
divide   succeed

Spelling:
proceed   provide

Earth

MAKE WORDS

at
rat
hat
ate/eat
ear
hear
tear/rate
hate/heat
heart/Earth

SORT WORDS

Rhymes:

at	ate	eat	ear
rat	rate	heat	hear
hat	hate		tear

TRANSFER WORDS

Reading:
defeat   format

Spelling:
combat   unclear

Make Words: Tell children how many letters to use to make each word. (A slash in the Make Words list indicates that words can be made with the same letters. An underline __ in the letter bank or on the letter strip indicates that a blank space is needed for the secret place.)

Emphasize how changing just one letter or rearranging letters makes different words:

"Add a letter to **ear** to spell **hear**."

"Change 1 letter in **rat** to spell **hat**."

"Use the same letters in **tear** to spell **rate**."

When children are not just adding or changing one letter, cue them to start over.

"Start over and use 3 letters to spell **ate**."

Give meaning or sentence clues when needed to clarify the word they are making:

"Change 1 letter in **hear** to spell **tear**. The girl wiped a **tear** from her eye as she watched the sad movie."

Give children one minute to figure out the secret words and then give clues if needed.

"Today's letters will make two secret words. The first one is not a place, but the other one is. One secret word is the part of your body that pumps blood. The other secret word is the name of the planet we live on."

Sort Rhymes

Reading Transfer: "Pretend you are reading and come to a new word." Have children put the words under the appropriate rhymes and use the rhymes to decode them.

Spelling Transfer: "Pretend you are writing and need to spell these words." Have children tell you how the words begin. Then, have children find and use the appropriate rhymes to finish spelling the new words.

Step-by-step directions for a sample *Making Places* lesson are on pages 9–13.

England

Make Words: Tell children how many letters to use to make each word. (A slash in the Make Words list indicates that words can be made with the same letters. An underline __ in the letter bank or on the letter strip indicates that a blank space is needed for the secret place.)

Emphasize how changing just one letter or rearranging letters makes different words:

"Add a letter to **end** to spell **lend**."

"Change 1 letter in **Dean** to spell **deal**."

"Use the same letters in **angel** to spell **angle**."

When children are not just adding or changing one letter, cue them to start over.

"Start over and use 5 new letters to spell **angel**."

Give meaning or sentence clues when needed to clarify the word they are making:

"Change 1 letter to spell **gale**. The hurricane brought **gale** force winds all along the coast."

Always alert children when they are making a name and expect them to use a capital letter.

"Take 4 letters and spell the name **Dale**."

Give children one minute to figure out the secret place and then give clues if needed.

"Our secret place is the name of a country that starts with **E**."

Sort Rhymes

Reading Transfer: "Pretend you are reading and come to a new word." Have children put the words under the appropriate rhymes and use the rhymes to decode them.

Spelling Transfer: "Pretend you are writing and need to spell these words." Have children tell you how the words begin. Then, have children find and use the appropriate rhymes to finish spelling the new words.

Step-by-step directions for a sample *Making Places* lesson are on pages 9–13.

MAKE WORDS

and
end
lend
lead
land
Dale
gale
lean
Dean
deal
angel/angle
dangle
England

SORT WORDS

Rhymes:

angle	and	end	Dale
dangle	land	lend	gale

lean
Dean

TRANSFER WORDS

Reading:
suspend   exhale

Spelling:
tangle   pretend

Florida

MAKE WORDS

air
aid
raid
road
load
rail
Ford®
lord
idol
fail
fair
flair/frail
radio
Florida

SORT WORDS

Rhymes:

rail	aid	air	road
fail	raid	fair	load
frail		flair	

Ford®
lord

TRANSFER WORDS

Reading:
afford   mermaid

Spelling:
repaid   unfair

Make Words: Tell children how many letters to use to make each word. (A slash in the Make Words list indicates that words can be made with the same letters. An underline __ in the letter bank or on the letter strip indicates that a blank space is needed for the secret place.)

Emphasize how changing just one letter or rearranging letters makes different words:

> "Add a letter to **fair** to spell **flair**."

> "Change 1 letter in **fail** to spell **fair**."

> "Use the same letters in **flair** to spell **frail**."

When children are not just adding or changing one letter, cue them to start over.

> "Start over and use 5 new letters to spell **radio**."

Give meaning or sentence clues when needed to clarify the word they are making:

> "Start over and use 4 letters to spell **idol**. Who is your **idol**—the person you admire most?"

Always alert children when they are making a name and expect them to use a capital letter.

> "Take 4 letters and spell **Ford**. Henry **Ford** built some of the first American cars."

Give children one minute to figure out the secret place and then give clues if needed.

> "Our secret place is the name of a state that starts with **F**."

Sort Rhymes

Reading Transfer: "Pretend you are reading and come to a new word." Have children put the words under the appropriate rhymes and use the rhymes to decode them.

Spelling Transfer: "Pretend you are writing and need to spell these words." Have children tell you how the words begin. Then, have children find and use the appropriate rhymes to finish spelling the new words.

Step-by-step directions for a sample *Making Places* lesson are on pages 9–13.

Georgia

Make Words: Tell children how many letters to use to make each word. (A slash in the Make Words list indicates that words can be made with the same letters. An underline __ in the letter bank or on the letter strip indicates that a blank space is needed for the secret place.)

Emphasize how changing just one letter or rearranging letters makes different words:

> "Change 1 letter in **rig** to spell **rag**."

> "Use the same letters in **ear** to spell **are**."

When children are not just adding or changing one letter, cue them to start over.

> "Start over and use 3 new letters to spell **egg**."

Give meaning or sentence clues when needed to clarify the word they are making:

> "Add 1 letter to spell **ago**. My grandparents came to this country a long time **ago**."

Always alert children when they are making a name and expect them to use a capital letter.

> "Take 4 letters and spell the name **Greg**."

Give children one minute to figure out the secret place and then give clues if needed.

> "Our secret place is the name of a state that starts with **G**."

Sort Related Words

Sort Rhymes

Reading Transfer: "Pretend you are reading and come to a new word." Have children put the words under the appropriate rhymes and use the rhymes to decode them.

Spelling Transfer: "Pretend you are writing and need to spell these words." Have children tell you how the words begin. Then, have children find and use the appropriate rhymes to finish spelling the new words.

Step-by-step directions for a sample *Making Places* lesson are on pages 9–13.

MAKE WORDS

go
ago
age
egg
air
ear/are
rig
rag
gag
rage/gear
Greg
Georgia

SORT WORDS

Related Words:
go, ago

Rhymes:

age	ear	rag
rage	gear	gag

TRANSFER WORDS

Reading:
appear   rampage

Spelling:
engage   zigzag

Germany

a e g m n r y

MAKE WORDS

gym
gem
germ
gear
year
name
game
angry
anger/range
manger/German
Germany

SORT WORDS

G Words with J Sound:
gym, gem, germ, range,
manger, German, Germany

Related Words:
German, Germany

Rhymes:
gear   name
year   game

TRANSFER WORDS

Reading:
endear   became

Spelling:
unclear   inflame

Make Words: Tell children how many letters to use to make each word. (A slash in the Make Words list indicates that words can be made with the same letters. An underline __ in the letter bank or on the letter strip indicates that a blank space is needed for the secret place.)

Emphasize how changing just one letter or rearranging letters makes different words:

"Add a letter to **gem** to spell **germ**."

"Change 1 letter in **name** to spell **game**."

"Use the same letters in **anger** to spell **range**."

When children are not just adding or changing one letter, cue them to start over.

"Start over and use 5 new letters to spell **angry**."

Give meaning or sentence clues when needed to clarify the word they are making:

"Use the same 6 letters to spell **German**. There are many **German** people living in our neighborhood."

Give children one minute to figure out the secret place and then give clues if needed.

"Our secret place is the name of a country that starts with **G**."

Sort G Words with J Sound

Sort Related Words

Sort Rhymes

Reading Transfer: "Pretend you are reading and come to a new word." Have children put the words under the appropriate rhymes and use the rhymes to decode them.

Spelling Transfer: "Pretend you are writing and need to spell these words." Have children tell you how the words begin. Then, have children find and use the appropriate rhymes to finish spelling the new words.

Step-by-step directions for a sample *Making Places* lesson are on pages 9–13.

Making Places • CD-104108 • © Carson-Dellosa

Great Britain

a a e i i b g n r r t t __

Make Words: Tell children how many letters to use to make each word. (A slash in the Make Words list indicates that words can be made with the same letters. An underline __ in the letter bank or on the letter strip indicates that a blank space is needed for the secret place.)

Emphasize how changing just one letter or rearranging letters makes different words:

> "Add a letter to **rainier** to spell **brainier**."

> "Use the same letters in **grate** to spell a different **great**. That was a **great** movie!"

When children are not just adding or changing one letter, cue them to start over.

> "Start over and use 5 new letters to spell **anger**."

Give meaning or sentence clues when needed to clarify the word they are making:

> "Add 1 letter to **gate** to spell **grate**. We are going to **grate** some cheese over the pizza."

Always alert children when they are making a name and expect them to use a capital letter.

> "Take 7 letters and spell the country of **Nigeria**."

Give children one minute to figure out the secret place and then give clues if needed.

> "Our secret place is an island that includes Scotland, England, and Wales."

Sort Homophones

Sort Related Words

Sort Rhymes

Reading Transfer: "Pretend you are reading and come to a new word." Have children put the words under the appropriate rhymes and use the rhymes to decode them.

Spelling Transfer: "Pretend you are writing and need to spell these words." Have children tell you how the words begin. Then, have children find and use the appropriate rhymes to finish spelling the new words.

Step-by-step directions for a sample *Making Places* lesson are on pages 9–13.

MAKE WORDS

- rain
- rate
- gate
- grate/great
- brain
- anger
- Nigeria
- angrier
- rainier
- brainier
- Great Britain

SORT WORDS

Homophones:
grate, great

Related Words:
rain, rainier; brain, brainier; anger, angrier

Rhymes:

rain	rainier	rate
brain	brainier	gate
		grate

TRANSFER WORDS

Reading:
inmate   complain

Spelling:
remain   donate

Greenland

a e e d g l n n r

MAKE WORDS

age
rage
green
large
angel/angle
dangle
danger/garden
enrage
enlarge/general
England
endanger
Greenland

SORT WORDS

Related Words:
rage, enrage; large, enlarge;
danger, endanger

Rhymes:
age   angle
rage   dangle

TRANSFER WORDS

Reading:
strangle   backstage

Spelling:
tangle   rampage

Make Words: Tell children how many letters to use to make each word. (A slash in the Make Words list indicates that words can be made with the same letters. An underline __ in the letter bank or on the letter strip indicates that a blank space is needed for the secret place.)

Emphasize how changing just one letter or rearranging letters makes different words:

"Add a letter to **angle** to spell **dangle**."

"Use the same letters in **enlarge** to spell **general**."

When children are not just adding or changing one letter, cue them to start over.

"Start over and use 6 new letters to spell **enrage**."

Give meaning or sentence clues when needed to clarify the word they are making:

"Use 7 letters to spell **enlarge**. The father chose his two favorite photographs to **enlarge**, frame, and hang on his office wall."

Always alert children when they are making a name and expect them to use a capital letter.

"Take 7 letters and spell the country of **England**."

Give children one minute to figure out the secret place and then give clues if needed.

"Our secret place is the name of an island that is a compound word, and we made one of the words."

Sort Related Words

Sort Rhymes

Reading Transfer: "Pretend you are reading and come to a new word." Have children put the words under the appropriate rhymes and use the rhymes to decode them.

Spelling Transfer: "Pretend you are writing and need to spell these words." Have children tell you how the words begin. Then, have children find and use the appropriate rhymes to finish spelling the new words.

Step-by-step directions for a sample *Making Places* lesson are on pages 9–13.

Making Places • CD-104108 • © Carson-Dellosa

Helena, Montana

a a a e e o h l m n n n t, __

Make Words: Tell children how many letters to use to make each word. (A slash in the Make Words list indicates that words can be made with the same letters. An underline __ in the letter bank or on the letter strip indicates that a blank space is needed for the secret place.)

Emphasize how changing just one letter or rearranging letters makes different words:

> "Change 1 letter in **late** to spell **hate**."

> "Add 1 letter to **metal** to spell **mental**."

> "Use the same letters in **hate** to spell **heat**."

When children are not just adding or changing one letter, cue them to start over.

> "Start over and use 5 new letters to spell **hotel**."

Always alert children when they are making a name and expect them to use a capital letter.

> "Take 7 letters and spell the state of **Montana**."

Give meaning or sentence clues when needed to clarify the word they are making:

> "Change one letter to spell a different **meet**. What time should we **meet**?"

Give children one minute to figure out the secret place and then give clues if needed.

> "Our secret place is a capital and its state, and we already spelled the state."

Sort Homophones

Sort Related Words

Sort Rhymes

Reading Transfer: "Pretend you are reading and come to a new word." Have children put the words under the appropriate rhymes and use the rhymes to decode them.

Spelling Transfer: "Pretend you are writing and need to spell these words." Have children tell you how the words begin. Then, have children find and use the appropriate rhymes to finish spelling the new words.

Step-by-step directions for a sample *Making Places* lesson are on pages 9–13.

MAKE WORDS

late
hate/heat
meat
meet
Helen
hotel
metal
mental
Montana
antenna
nonmetal
Helena, Montana

SORT WORDS

Homophones:
meat, meet

Related Words:
metal, nonmetal

Rhymes:
late   heat
hate   meat

TRANSFER WORDS

Reading:
mistreat   translate

Spelling:
update   locate

Honolulu, Hawaii

a a i i o o u u h h l l n w , __

MAKE WORDS

now
how
hill
will
wall
hall
haul
Ohio
Iowa
aloha
allow
hollow
Hawaii
Honolulu, Hawaii

SORT WORDS

Homophones:
hall, haul

Rhymes:
hill   wall
will   hall

TRANSFER WORDS

Reading:
treadmill   meatball

Spelling:
snowfall   standstill

Make Words: Tell children how many letters to use to make each word. (A slash in the Make Words list indicates that words can be made with the same letters. An underline __ in the letter bank or on the letter strip indicates that a blank space is needed for the secret place.)

Emphasize how changing just one letter or rearranging letters makes different words:

> "Change 1 letter in **hill** to spell **will**."

When children are not just adding or changing one letter, cue them to start over.

> "Start over and use 5 new letters to spell **aloha**."

Always alert children when they are making a name and expect them to use a capital letter.

> "Take 6 letters and spell the state of **Hawaii**."

Give meaning or sentence clues when needed to clarify the word they are making:

> "Change 1 letter in **hall** to spell a word that sounds exactly the same as **hall**. We filled the dumpster and a truck came to **haul** it away."

Give children one minute to figure out the secret place and then give clues if needed.

> "Our secret place is a capital and its state, and we already spelled the state."

Sort Homophones

Sort Rhymes

Reading Transfer: "Pretend you are reading and come to a new word." Have children put the words under the appropriate rhymes and use the rhymes to decode them.

Spelling Transfer: "Pretend you are writing and need to spell these words." Have children tell you how the words begin. Then, have children find and use the appropriate rhymes to finish spelling the new words.

Step-by-step directions for a sample *Making Places* lesson are on pages 9–13.

Houston

Make Words: Tell children how many letters to use to make each word. (A slash in the Make Words list indicates that words can be made with the same letters. An underline __ in the letter bank or on the letter strip indicates that a blank space is needed for the secret place.)

Emphasize how changing just one letter or rearranging letters makes different words:

"Add a letter to **hoot** to spell **shoot**."

"Change 1 letter in **snout** to spell **shout**."

"Use the same letters in **shout** to spell **south**."

When children are not just adding or changing one letter, cue them to start over.

"Start over and use 4 letters to spell **hoot**."

Give meaning or sentence clues when needed to clarify the word they are making:

"Change 1 letter spell a different **son**. The family had two daughters and one **son**."

Give children one minute to figure out the secret place and then give clues if needed.

"Our secret place is a city in Texas that begins with **H**."

Sort Homophones

Sort Rhymes

Reading Transfer: "Pretend you are reading and come to a new word." Have children put the words under the appropriate rhymes and use the rhymes to decode them.

Spelling Transfer: "Pretend you are writing and need to spell these words." Have children tell you how the words begin. Then, have children find and use the appropriate rhymes to finish spelling the new words.

Step-by-step directions for a sample *Making Places* lesson are on pages 9–13.

MAKE WORDS

sun
son
out
not
hot
hut
nut
hoot
shoot
snout
shout/south
Houston

SORT WORDS

Homophones:
sun, son

Rhymes:

hut	out	not	hoot
nut	snout	hot	shoot
	shout		

TRANSFER WORDS

Reading:
haircut   mascot

Spelling:
forgot   dugout

Hungary

MAKE WORDS

rag
hag
hay
Ray
gray
rang
hang
hung
rung
angry
hungry
Hungary

SORT WORDS

Rhymes:

rag	hay	rang	hung
hag	Ray	hang	rung
	gray		

TRANSFER WORDS

Reading:
holiday   boomerang

Spelling:
gangway   yesterday

Make Words: Tell children how many letters to use to make each word. (A slash in the Make Words list indicates that words can be made with the same letters. An underline __ in the letter bank or on the letter strip indicates that a blank space is needed for the secret place.)

Emphasize how changing just one letter or rearranging letters makes different words:

"Add a letter to **Ray** to spell **gray**."

"Change 1 letter in **hag** to spell **hay**."

When children are not just adding or changing one letter, cue them to start over.

"Start over and use 5 new letters to spell **angry**."

Give meaning or sentence clues when needed to clarify the word they are making:

"Change 1 letter to spell **rung**. The bottom **rung** of the ladder broke."

Always alert children when they are making a name and expect them to use a capital letter.

"Change 1 letter and spell the name **Ray**."

Give children one minute to figure out the secret place and then give clues if needed.

"Our secret place is the name of a country that starts with **H**."

Sort Rhymes

Reading Transfer: "Pretend you are reading and come to a new word." Have children put the words under the appropriate rhymes and use the rhymes to decode them.

Spelling Transfer: "Pretend you are writing and need to spell these words." Have children tell you how the words begin. Then, have children find and use the appropriate rhymes to finish spelling the new words.

Step-by-step directions for a sample *Making Places* lesson are on pages 9–13.

Illinois

i i i o l l n s

Make Words: Tell children how many letters to use to make each word. (A slash in the Make Words list indicates that words can be made with the same letters. An underline __ in the letter bank or on the letter strip indicates that a blank space is needed for the secret place.)

Emphasize how changing just one letter or rearranging letters makes different words:

"Add a letter to **ill** to spell **sill**."

"Use the same letters in **soil** to spell **silo**."

When children are not just adding or changing one letter, cue them to start over.

"Start over and use 5 new letters to spell **lions**."

Give meaning or sentence clues when needed to clarify the word they are making:

"Use the same letters to spell **loins**. At the cookout, they barbecued pork **loins**."

Always alert children when they are making a name and expect them to use a capital letter.

"Use the same letters and spell the name **Lois**."

Give children one minute to figure out the secret place and then give clues if needed.

"Our secret place is the name of a state that starts with **I**."

Sort Related Words

Sort Rhymes

Reading Transfer: "Pretend you are reading and come to a new word." Have children put the words under the appropriate rhymes and use the rhymes to decode them.

Spelling Transfer: "Pretend you are writing and need to spell these words." Have children tell you how the words begin. Then, have children find and use the appropriate rhymes to finish spelling the new words.

Step-by-step directions for a sample *Making Places* lesson are on pages 9–13.

MAKE WORDS

in
son
oil
ill
sill
soil/silo/Lois/oils
lions/loins
Illinois

SORT WORDS

Related Words:
oil, oils

Rhymes:
oil   ill
soil   sill

TRANSFER WORDS

Reading:
anthill   turmoil

Spelling:
recoil   downhill

Indiana

a a i i d n n

MAKE WORDS

in
an
ad
aid
and/Dan
Nan
Anna
Nina
Dina
Diana
India
Indian
Indiana

SORT WORDS

Related Words:
India, Indian

Rhymes:
an   Nina
Dan   Dina
Nan

TRANSFER WORDS

Reading:
Gina   caravan

Spelling:
Tina   minivan

Make Words: Tell children how many letters to use to make each word. (A slash in the Make Words list indicates that words can be made with the same letters. An underline __ in the letter bank or on the letter strip indicates that a blank space is needed for the secret place.)

Emphasize how changing just one letter or rearranging letters makes different words:

"Add a letter to **ad** to spell **aid**."

"Change 1 letter in **Dan** to spell the name **Nan**."

"Use the same letters in **and** to spell the name **Dan**."

When children are not just adding or changing one letter, cue them to start over.

"Add 1 letter to spell the name **Diana**."

Give meaning or sentence clues when needed to clarify the word they are making:

"Add 1 letter to spell **Indian**. The **Indian** restaurant serves the kind of food people eat in India."

Always alert children when they are making a name and expect them to use a capital letter.

"Take 5 letters and spell the country of **India**."

Give children one minute to figure out the secret place and then give clues if needed.

"Our secret place is the name of a state that starts with **I**."

Sort Related Words

Sort Rhymes

Reading Transfer: "Pretend you are reading and come to a new word." Have children put the words under the appropriate rhymes and use the rhymes to decode them.

Spelling Transfer: "Pretend you are writing and need to spell these words." Have children tell you how the words begin. Then, have children find and use the appropriate rhymes to finish spelling the new words.

Step-by-step directions for a sample *Making Places* lesson are on pages 9–13.

Indianapolis

a a i i i o d l n n p s

Make Words: Tell children how many letters to use to make each word. (A slash in the Make Words list indicates that words can be made with the same letters. An underline __ in the letter bank or on the letter strip indicates that a blank space is needed for the secret place.)

Emphasize how changing just one letter or rearranging letters makes different words:

"Add a letter to **pain** to spell **plain**."

When children are not just adding or changing one letter, cue them to start over.

"Start over and use 5 new letters to spell **panda**."

Give meaning or sentence clues when needed to clarify the word they are making:

"Start over and use 5 letters to spell the country of **India**. **India** is a large country in Asia."

Always alert children when they are making a name and expect them to use a capital letter.

"Take 4 letters and spell the country of **Laos**."

Give children one minute to figure out the secret place and then give clues if needed.

"Our secret place is the capital of Indiana."

Sort Related Words

Sort Rhymes

Reading Transfer: "Pretend you are reading and come to a new word." Have children put the words under the appropriate rhymes and use the rhymes to decode them.

Spelling Transfer: "Pretend you are writing and need to spell these words." Have children tell you how the words begin. Then, have children find and use the appropriate rhymes to finish spelling the new words.

Step-by-step directions for a sample *Making Places* lesson are on pages 9–13.

MAKE WORDS

pan
span
plan
Laos
pain
plain
Spain
salad
panda
India
Indian
island
Poland
Indiana
Indianapolis

SORT WORDS

Related Words:
India, Indian

Rhymes:
pan	pain
span	plain
plan	Spain

TRANSFER WORDS

Reading:
complain   restrain

Spelling:
maintain   explain

Indian Ocean

a a e i i o c d n n __

MAKE WORDS

one
once
none
nine
dine
Diana
Donna
dance
canoe/ocean
India
cannon
Indian
Indiana
Indian Ocean

SORT WORDS

Related Words:
one, once

Rhymes:
one   nine
none   dine

TRANSFER WORDS

Reading:
decline   confine

Spelling:
recline   define

Make Words: Tell children how many letters to use to make each word. (A slash in the Make Words list indicates that words can be made with the same letters. An underline __ in the letter bank or on the letter strip indicates that a blank space is needed for the secret place.)

Emphasize how changing just one letter or rearranging letters makes different words:

"Add a letter to **one** to spell **once**."

"Change 1 letter in **nine** to spell **dine**."

When children are not just adding or changing one letter, cue them to start over.

"Start over and use 5 new letters to spell **canoe**."

Give meaning or sentence clues when needed to clarify the word they are making:

"Add 1 letter to spell **Indiana**. **Indiana** is a state in the Midwest."

Always alert children when they are making a name and expect them to use a capital letter.

"Take 5 letters and spell the country of **India**."

Give children one minute to figure out the secret place and then give clues if needed.

"Our secret place is an ocean with two words in its name."

Sort Related Words

Sort Rhymes

Reading Transfer: "Pretend you are reading and come to a new word." Have children put the words under the appropriate rhymes and use the rhymes to decode them.

Spelling Transfer: "Pretend you are writing and need to spell these words." Have children tell you how the words begin. Then, have children find and use the appropriate rhymes to finish spelling the new words.

Step-by-step directions for a sample *Making Places* lesson are on pages 9–13.

Making Places • CD-104108 • © Carson-Dellosa

Indonesia

Make Words: Tell children how many letters to use to make each word. (A slash in the Make Words list indicates that words can be made with the same letters. An underline __ in the letter bank or on the letter strip indicates that a blank space is needed for the secret place.)

Emphasize how changing just one letter or rearranging letters makes different words:

"Add a letter to **nose** to spell **noise**."

"Change 1 letter in **send** to spell **sand**."

"Use the same letters in **ideas** to spell **aside**."

When children are not just adding or changing one letter, cue them to start over.

"Start over and use 5 new letters to spell **ideas**."

Give meaning or sentence clues when needed to clarify the word they are making:

"Use 4 letters to spell **sane**. The accused was pronounced **sane** and able to stand trial."

Always alert children when they are making a name and expect them to use a capital letter.

"Take 5 letters and spell the country of **India**."

Give children one minute to figure out the secret place and then give clues if needed.

"Our secret place is the name of a country that starts with **I**."

Sort Related Words

Sort Rhymes

Reading Transfer: "Pretend you are reading and come to a new word." Have children put the words under the appropriate rhymes and use the rhymes to decode them.

Spelling Transfer: "Pretend you are writing and need to spell these words." Have children tell you how the words begin. Then, have children find and use the appropriate rhymes to finish spelling the new words.

Step-by-step directions for a sample *Making Places* lesson are on pages 9–13.

MAKE WORDS

and
end
send
sand
sane
side
nose
noise
ideas/aside
India
inside
insane
Indians
Indonesia

SORT WORDS

Related Words:
India, Indians; sane, insane; side, aside, inside

Rhymes:
and   end
sand   send

TRANSFER WORDS

Reading:
dividend   Thailand

Spelling:
understand   pretend

Ireland

► MAKE WORDS

nail
rail
earn
Iran
lean
lead/deal
ideal
learn
alien
derail
Daniel/nailed/denial
Ireland

► SORT WORDS

Related Words:
rail, derail; nail, nailed

Rhymes:
earn   nail
learn   rail

► TRANSFER WORDS

Reading:
monorail   prevail

Spelling:
detail   fingernail

Make Words: Tell children how many letters to use to make each word. (A slash in the Make Words list indicates that words can be made with the same letters. An underline __ in the letter bank or on the letter strip indicates that a blank space is needed for the secret place.)

Emphasize how changing just one letter or rearranging letters makes different words:

> "Add a letter to **deal** to spell **ideal**."

> "Change 1 letter in **nail** to spell **rail**."

> "Use the same letters in **Daniel** to spell **nailed**. Use the letters again to spell **denial**."

When children are not just adding or changing one letter, cue them to start over.

> "Start over and use 5 new letters to spell **learn**."

Give meaning or sentence clues when needed to clarify the word they are making:

> "Start over and use 5 letters to spell **alien**. The movie was about an **alien** who came here from another planet."

Always alert children when they are making a name and expect them to use a capital letter.

> "Take 6 letters and spell the name **Daniel**."

Give children one minute to figure out the secret place and then give clues if needed.

> "Our secret place is the name of a country that starts with **I**."

Sort Related Words

Sort Rhymes

Reading Transfer: "Pretend you are reading and come to a new word." Have children put the words under the appropriate rhymes and use the rhymes to decode them.

Spelling Transfer: "Pretend you are writing and need to spell these words." Have children tell you how the words begin. Then, have children find and use the appropriate rhymes to finish spelling the new words.

Step-by-step directions for a sample *Making Places* lesson are on pages 9–13.

islands

a i d l n s s

Make Words: Tell children how many letters to use to make each word. (A slash in the Make Words list indicates that words can be made with the same letters. An underline __ in the letter bank or on the letter strip indicates that a blank space is needed for the secret place.)

Emphasize how changing just one letter or rearranging letters makes different words:

> "Add a letter to **lid** to spell **slid**."

> "Change 1 letter in **land** to spell **sand**."

> "Use the same letters in **nails** to spell **snail**."

When children are not just adding or changing one letter, cue them to start over.

> "Start over and use 4 letters to spell **sail**."

Give meaning or sentence clues when needed to clarify the word they are making:

> "Use the same 5 letters to spell **snail**. The **snail** got squished when I stepped on it."

Give children one minute to figure out the secret place and then give clues if needed.

> "Our secret place refers to bits of land completely surrounded by water."

Sort Rhymes

Reading Transfer: "Pretend you are reading and come to a new word." Have children put the words under the appropriate rhymes, and use the rhymes to decode them.

Spelling Transfer: "Pretend you are writing and need to spell these words." Have children tell you how the words begin. Then, have children find and use the appropriate rhymes to finish spelling the new words.

Step-by-step directions for a sample *Making Places* lesson are on pages 9–13.

MAKE WORDS

and
lid
slid
land
sand
sail
nail
nails/snail
islands

SORT WORDS

Rhymes:
and	nail	lid
land	snail	slid
sand		

TRANSFER WORDS

Reading:
Thailand   Madrid

Spelling:
headband   toenail

Israel

MAKE WORDS

is
Al
Sal
Ira
are/ear
rail
sail
sale/seal
real
Israel

SORT WORDS

Homophones:
sail, sale

Rhymes:
seal   rail
real   sail

TRANSFER WORDS

Reading:
conceal   ordeal

Spelling:
reveal   appeal

Make Words: Tell children how many letters to use to make each word. (A slash in the Make Words list indicates that words can be made with the same letters. An underline __ in the letter bank or on the letter strip indicates that a blank space is needed for the secret place.)

Emphasize how changing just one letter or rearranging letters makes different words:

"Add a letter to **Al** to spell the name **Sal**."

"Change 1 letter in **rail** to spell **sail**."

"Use the same letters in **sale** to spell **seal**."

When children are not just adding or changing one letter, cue them to start over.

"Start over and use 4 new letters to spell **rail**."

Give meaning or sentence clues when needed to clarify the word they are making:

"Use 4 letters to spell another word that sounds exactly like **sail**. On Friday, I went to the grocery store becaue they were having a **sale** on orange juice."

Always alert children when they are making a name and expect them to use a capital letter.

"Start over and use 3 letters and spell the name **Ira**."

Give children one minute to figure out the secret place and then give clues if needed.

"Our secret place is the name of a country that starts with **I**."

Sort Homophones

Sort Rhymes

Reading Transfer: "Pretend you are reading and come to a new word." Have children put the words under the appropriate rhymes and use the rhymes to decode them.

Spelling Transfer: "Pretend you are writing and need to spell these words." Have children tell you how the words begin. Then, have children find and use the appropriate rhymes to finish spelling the new words.

Step-by-step directions for a sample *Making Places* lesson are on pages 9–13.

70

Jackson

a o c j k n s

Make Words: Tell children how many letters to use to make each word. (A slash in the Make Words list indicates that words can be made with the same letters. An underline __ in the letter bank or on the letter strip indicates that a blank space is needed for the secret place.)

Emphasize how changing just one letter or rearranging letters makes different words:

> "Add a letter to **oak** to spell **soak**."

> "Change 1 letter in **Jan** to spell **can**."

When children are not just adding or changing one letter, cue them to start over.

> "Start over and use 4 letters to spell **sock**."

Give meaning or sentence clues when needed to clarify the word they are making:

> "Use 4 letters to spell **scan**. We are going to **scan** the pictures into the computer for our report."

Always alert children when they are making a name and expect them to use a capital letter.

> "Use 5 letters and spell the name **Jason**."

Give children one minute to figure out the secret place and then give clues if needed.

> "Our secret place is the capital of Mississippi and begins with a **J**."

Sort Rhymes

Reading Transfer: "Pretend you are reading and come to a new word." Have children put the words under the appropriate rhymes and use the rhymes to decode them.

Spelling Transfer: "Pretend you are writing and need to spell these words." Have children tell you how the words begin. Then, have children find and use the appropriate rhymes to finish spelling the new words.

Step-by-step directions for a sample *Making Places* lesson are on pages 9–13.

MAKE WORDS

Jan
can
oak
soak
scan
Jack
sack
snack
sock
jock
Jason
Jackson

SORT WORDS

Rhymes:

Jack	Jan	oak	sock
sack	can	soak	jock
snack	scan		

TRANSFER WORDS

Reading:
shamrock   attack

Spelling:
racetrack   roadblock

Jefferson City

e e i o c f f j n r s t y __

MAKE WORDS

toy
joy
city
fort
sort
sore
core
score
force
reject
rejoice
enforce
fortify
rejection
Jefferson City

SORT WORDS

Related Words:
fort, fortify; joy, rejoice;
force, enforce;
reject, rejection

Rhymes:

sore	fort	toy
core	sort	joy
score		

TRANSFER WORDS

Reading:
annoy   explore

Spelling:
restore   destroy

Make Words: Tell children how many letters to use to make each word. (A slash in the Make Words list indicates that words can be made with the same letters. An underline __ in the letter bank or on the letter strip indicates that a blank space is needed for the secret place.)

Emphasize how changing just one letter or rearranging letters makes different words:

> "Add a letter to **core** to spell **score**."

> "Change 1 letter in **fort** to spell **sort**."

When children are not just adding or changing one letter, cue them to start over.

> "Start over and use 7 new letters to spell **enforce**."

Give meaning or sentence clues when needed to clarify the word they are making:

> "Use 9 letters to spell **rejection**. My brother couldn't go into the army because of a leg injury, and he was very disappointed by his **rejection**."

Give children one minute to figure out the secret place and then give clues if needed.

> "Our secret place is the capital of Missouri, and the first word begins with **J**."

Sort Related Words

Sort Rhymes

Reading Transfer: "Pretend you are reading and come to a new word." Have children put the words under the appropriate rhymes and use the rhymes to decode them.

Spelling Transfer: "Pretend you are writing and need to spell these words." Have children tell you how the words begin. Then, have children find and use the appropriate rhymes to finish spelling the new words.

Step-by-step directions for a sample *Making Places* lesson are on pages 9–13.

Making Places • CD-104108 • © Carson-Dellosa

Jerusalem

a e e u j l m r s

Make Words: Tell children how many letters to use to make each word. (A slash in the Make Words list indicates that words can be made with the same letters. An underline __ in the letter bank or on the letter strip indicates that a blank space is needed for the secret place.)

Emphasize how changing just one letter or rearranging letters makes different words:

> "Add a letter to **us** to spell **use**."

> "Change 1 letter in **male** to spell **mule**."

When children are not just adding or changing one letter, cue them to start over.

> "Start over and use 5 new letters to spell **erase**."

Give meaning or sentence clues when needed to clarify the word they are making:

> "Use 5 letters to spell **laser**. My grandma had **laser** surgery on her eyes."

Always alert children when they are making a name and expect them to use a capital letter.

> "Use 5 letters and spell the city of **Salem**. **Salem** is the capital of Oregon."

Give children one minute to figure out the secret place and then give clues if needed.

> "Our secret place is a city in Israel that begins with **J**."

Sort Rhymes

Reading Transfer: "Pretend you are reading and come to a new word." Have children put the words under the appropriate rhymes and use the rhymes to decode them.

Spelling Transfer: "Pretend you are writing and need to spell these words." Have children tell you how the words begin. Then, have children find and use the appropriate rhymes to finish spelling the new words.

Step-by-step directions for a sample *Making Places* lesson are on pages 9–13.

MAKE WORDS

us
use
sale
male
mule
rule
mural
erase
laser
Salem
Jerusalem

SORT WORDS

Rhymes:
| sale | mule |
| male | rule |

TRANSFER WORDS

Reading:
upscale   molecule

Spelling:
inhale   overrule

Juneau, Alaska

aaaaeuujklns, __

MAKE WORDS

June
Jane/Jean
lean/lane
lake/leak
Jake
snake/sneak
Alaska
Juneau, Alaska

SORT WORDS

Rhymes:

Jane	Jean	leak	lake
lane	lean	sneak	Jake
			snake

TRANSFER WORDS

Reading:
earthquake   hurricane

Spelling:
pancake   airplane

Make Words: Tell children how many letters to use to make each word. (A slash in the Make Words list indicates that words can be made with the same letters. An underline __ in the letter bank or on the letter strip indicates that a blank space is needed for the secret place.)

Emphasize how changing just one letter or rearranging letters makes different words:

> "Change 1 letter in **June** to spell the name **Jane**."

> "Use the same letters in **snake** to spell **sneak**."

Give meaning or sentence clues when needed to clarify the word they are making:

> "Change 1 letter to spell **lean**. We always buy **lean** steaks that don't have a lot of fat."

Always alert children when they are making a name and expect them to use a capital letter.

> "Use 6 letters and spell the state of **Alaska**."

Give children one minute to figure out the secret place and then give clues if needed.

> "Our secret place is a capital and a state, and we spelled the state."

Sort Rhymes

Reading Transfer: "Pretend you are reading and come to a new word." Have children put the words under the appropriate rhymes and use the rhymes to decode them.

Spelling Transfer: "Pretend you are writing and need to spell these words." Have children tell you how the words begin. Then, have children find and use the appropriate rhymes to finish spelling the new words.

Step-by-step directions for a sample *Making Places* lesson are on pages 9–13.

Making Places • CD-104108 • © Carson-Dellosa

Kansas City

a a i c k n s s t y __

Make Words: Tell children how many letters to use to make each word. (A slash in the Make Words list indicates that words can be made with the same letters. An underline __ in the letter bank or on the letter strip indicates that a blank space is needed for the secret place.)

Emphasize how changing just one letter or rearranging letters makes different words:

"Add a letter to **stink** to spell **stinky**."

"Change 1 letter in **stinky** to spell **sticky**."

When children are not just adding or changing one letter, cue them to start over.

"Start over and use 4 new letters to spell **city**."

Give children one minute to figure out the secret place and then give clues if needed.

"Our secret place is a city in both Kansas and Missouri."

Sort Rhymes

Reading Transfer: "Pretend you are reading and come to a new word." Have children put the words under the appropriate rhymes and use the rhymes to decode them.

Spelling Transfer: "Pretend you are writing and need to spell these words." Have children tell you how the words begin. Then, have children find and use the appropriate rhymes to finish spelling the new words.

Step-by-step directions for a sample *Making Places* lesson are on pages 9–13.

MAKE WORDS

kiss
city
sink
sick
stick
stack
snack
stink
stinky
sticky
Kansas
Kansas City

SORT WORDS

Rhymes:
stack   sink   sick
snack   stink   stick

TRANSFER WORDS

Reading:
yardstick   fullback

Spelling:
toothpick   backpack

Kentucky

MAKE WORDS

cut
nut
net/ten
yet
key
Ken
Kent
cent
neck
cute
tune
Kentucky

SORT WORDS

Rhymes:

net	cut	Kent
yet	nut	cent

TRANSFER WORDS

Reading:
consent   torment

Spelling:
event   prevent

Make Words: Tell children how many letters to use to make each word. (A slash in the Make Words list indicates that words can be made with the same letters. An underline __ in the letter bank or on the letter strip indicates that a blank space is needed for the secret place.)

Emphasize how changing just one letter or rearranging letters makes different words:

"Change 1 letter in **Kent** to spell **cent**."

"Add 1 letter to **Ken** to spell **Kent**."

"Use the same letters in **net** to spell **ten**."

When children are not just adding or changing one letter, cue them to start over.

"Start over and use 4 new letters to spell **neck**."

Give meaning or sentence clues when needed to clarify the word they are making:

"Start over and use 4 letters to spell **tune**. Before each concert, the musicians **tune** their instruments."

Always alert children when they are making a name and expect them to use a capital letter.

"Change 1 letter and spell the name **Ken**."

Give children one minute to figure out the secret place and then give clues if needed.

"Our secret place is the name of a state that starts with **K**."

Sort Rhymes

Reading Transfer: "Pretend you are reading and come to a new word." Have children put the words under the appropriate rhymes and use the rhymes to decode them.

Spelling Transfer: "Pretend you are writing and need to spell these words." Have children tell you how the words begin. Then, have children find and use the appropriate rhymes to finish spelling the new words.

Step-by-step directions for a sample *Making Places* lesson are on pages 9–13.

Lake Erie

a e e e i k l r __

Make Words: Tell children how many letters to use to make each word. (A slash in the Make Words list indicates that words can be made with the same letters. An underline __ in the letter bank or on the letter strip indicates that a blank space is needed for the secret place.)

Emphasize how changing just one letter or rearranging letters makes different words:

> "Add a letter to **like** to spell **alike**."

> "Change 1 letter in **rake** to spell **lake**."

> "Use the same letters in **lake** to spell **leak**."

When children are not just adding or changing one letter, cue them to start over.

> "Start over and use 4 new letters to spell **lark**."

Give meaning or sentence clues when needed to clarify the word they are making:

> "Change 1 letter to spell another word that sounds exactly like **reel** but is spelled differently. The book had lots of photos of **real** animals."

Always alert children when they are making a name and expect them to use a capital letter.

> "Use the same letters to spell the name **Kalie**."

Give children one minute to figure out the secret place and then give clues if needed.

> "Our secret place is a lake with two words in its name, and we made one of the words."

Sort Homophones

Sort Related Words

Sort Rhymes

Reading Transfer: "Pretend you are reading and come to a new word." Have children put the words under the appropriate rhymes and use the rhymes to decode them.

Spelling Transfer: "Pretend you are writing and need to spell these words." Have children tell you how the words begin. Then, have children find and use the appropriate rhymes to finish spelling the new words.

Step-by-step directions for a sample *Making Places* lesson are on pages 9–13.

MAKE WORDS

are
lie
eel
reel
real
lark
rake
lake/leak
like
alike/Kalie
Lake Erie

SORT WORDS

Homophones:
reel, real

Related Words:
like, alike

Rhymes:
| eel | rake |
| reel | lake |

TRANSFER WORDS

Reading:
handshake   earthquake

Spelling:
mistake   snowflake

Lake Huron

a e o u h l k n r _

MAKE WORDS

our
hour
Hank
rank
rake
lake
heal
real
earn
learn
Korea
Korean
unreal
Lake Huron

SORT WORDS

Homophones:
our, hour

Related Words:
real, unreal; Korea, Korean

Rhymes:

heal	earn	rake	Hank
real	learn	lake	rank

TRANSFER WORDS

Reading:
conceal   appeal

Spelling:
outrank   reveal

Make Words: Tell children how many letters to use to make each word. (A slash in the Make Words list indicates that words can be made with the same letters. An underline __ in the letter bank or on the letter strip indicates that a blank space is needed for the secret place.)

Emphasize how changing just one letter or rearranging letters makes different words:

> "Add a letter to **earn** to spell **learn**."

> "Change 1 letter in **Hank** to spell **rank**."

When children are not just adding or changing one letter, cue them to start over.

> "Start over and use 6 new letters to spell **unreal**."

Give meaning or sentence clues when needed to clarify the word they are making:

> "Add a letter to spell another word that sounds exactly like **our** but is spelled differently. I can watch one **hour** of TV."

Always alert children when they are making a name and expect them to use a capital letter.

> "Take 5 letters and spell the country of **Korea**. **Korea** used to be one country but was divided into South Korea and North Korea."

Give children one minute to figure out the secret place and then give clues if needed.

> "Our secret place is a lake with two words in its name, and we made one of the words."

Sort Homophones

Sort Related Words

Sort Rhymes

Reading Transfer: "Pretend you are reading and come to a new word." Have children put the words under the appropriate rhymes and use the rhymes to decode them.

Spelling Transfer: "Pretend you are writing and need to spell these words." Have children tell you how the words begin. Then, have children find and use the appropriate rhymes to finish spelling the new words.

Step-by-step directions for a sample *Making Places* lesson are on pages 9–13.

Lake Michigan

a a e i i c g h k l m n __

Make Words: Tell children how many letters to use to make each word. (A slash in the Make Words list indicates that words can be made with the same letters. An underline __ in the letter bank or on the letter strip indicates that a blank space is needed for the secret place.)

Emphasize how changing just one letter or rearranging letters makes different words:

"Add a letter to **ice** to spell **lice**."

"Change 1 letter in **lice** to spell **like**."

When children are not just adding or changing one letter, cue them to start over.

"Start over and use 5 new letters to spell **angel**."

Give meaning or sentence clues when needed to clarify the word they are making:

"Start over and use 7 letters to spell **angelic**. Everyone thought the new grandbaby looked **angelic**."

Always alert children when they are making a name and expect them to use a capital letter.

"Take 8 letters and spell the state of **Michigan**."

Give children one minute to figure out the secret place and then give clues if needed.

"Our secret place is a lake with two words in its name, and we made one of the words."

Sort Related Words

Sort Rhymes

Reading Transfer: "Pretend you are reading and come to a new word." Have children put the words under the appropriate rhymes and use the rhymes to decode them.

Spelling Transfer: "Pretend you are writing and need to spell these words." Have children tell you how the words begin. Then, have children find and use the appropriate rhymes to finish spelling the new words.

Step-by-step directions for a sample *Making Places* lesson are on pages 9–13.

MAKE WORDS

ice
lice
like
hike
magic
angel
Chile
hiking
machine
imagine
angelic
magical
magician
Michigan
Lake Michigan

SORT WORDS

Related Words:
angel, angelic;
magic, magical, magician

Rhymes:
ice   like
lice   hike

TRANSFER WORDS

Reading:
hitchhike   advice

Spelling:
alike   dislike

Lake Ontario

a a e i o o k l n r t __

MAKE WORDS

tank
rank
rink
link
root
loot
Karen
Korea
Korean
looter
Latino
Laotian
Ontario
Lake Ontario

SORT WORDS

Related Words:
loot, looter; Korea, Korean

Rhymes:
rink   root   tank
link   loot   rank

TRANSFER WORDS

Reading:
outrank   outshoot

Spelling:
uproot   overshoot

Make Words: Tell children how many letters to use to make each word. (A slash in the Make Words list indicates that words can be made with the same letters. An underline __ in the letter bank or on the letter strip indicates that a blank space is needed for the secret place.)

Emphasize how changing just one letter or rearranging letters makes different words:

> "Add a letter to **Korea** to spell **Korean**."

> "Change 1 letter in **rank** to spell **rink**."

When children are not just adding or changing one letter, cue them to start over.

> "Start over and use 6 new letters to spell **looter**."

Give meaning or sentence clues when needed to clarify the word they are making:

> "Start over and use 7 letters to spell **Laotian**. His **Laotian** grandparents were born in Laos."

Always alert children when they are making a name and expect them to use a capital letter.

> "Take 7 letters and spell **Ontario**. **Ontario** is a large city in Canada."

Give children one minute to figure out the secret place and then give clues if needed.

> "Our secret place is a lake with two words in its name, and we made one of the words."

Sort Related Words

Sort Rhymes

Reading Transfer: "Pretend you are reading and come to a new word." Have children put the words under the appropriate rhymes and use the rhymes to decode them.

Spelling Transfer: "Pretend you are writing and need to spell these words." Have children tell you how the words begin. Then, have children find and use the appropriate rhymes to finish spelling the new words.

Step-by-step directions for a sample *Making Places* lesson are on pages 9–13.

Lake Superior

a e e i o u k l p r r s _

Make Words: Tell children how many letters to use to make each word. (A slash in the Make Words list indicates that words can be made with the same letters. An underline __ in the letter bank or on the letter strip indicates that a blank space is needed for the secret place.)

Emphasize how changing just one letter or rearranging letters makes different words:

> "Add a letter to **peak** to spell **speak**."

> "Change 1 letter in **rake** to spell **lake**."

> "Use the same letters in **lake** to spell **leak**."

When children are not just adding or changing one letter, cue them to start over.

> "Start over and use 5 letters to spell **skier**."

Give meaning or sentence clues when needed to clarify the word they are making:

> "Start over and use 6 letters to spell **uproar**. When the lizard escaped, there was a huge **uproar** in the classroom."

Always alert children when they are making a name and expect them to use a capital letter.

> "Take 6 letters and spell the continent of **Europe**."

Give children one minute to figure out the secret place and then give clues if needed.

> "Our secret place is a lake with two words in its name, and we made both words."

Sort Related Words

Sort Rhymes

Reading Transfer: "Pretend you are reading and come to a new word." Have children put the words under the appropriate rhymes and use the rhymes to decode them.

Spelling Transfer: "Pretend you are writing and need to spell these words." Have children tell you how the words begin. Then, have children find and use the appropriate rhymes to finish spelling the new words.

Step-by-step directions for a sample *Making Places* lesson are on pages 9–13.

MAKE WORDS

ski
roar
rake
lake/leak
peak
speak
skier
Paris
uproar
Europe
please
speaker
pleasure
superior
Lake Superior

SORT WORDS

Related Words:
roar, uproar; ski, skier;
speak, speaker; please, pleasure

Rhymes:
peak   rake
speak   lake

TRANSFER WORDS

Reading:
rattlesnake   snowflake

Spelling:
pancake   awake

Las Vegas

a a e g l s s v __

MAKE WORDS

gal
gas/sag
lag
leg
seal/sale
gale
gave
save/vase
slave
glass
savage
Las Vegas

SORT WORDS

Rhymes:
gave   sag   sale
save   lag   gale
slave

TRANSFER WORDS

Reading:
enslave   engrave

Spelling:
forgave   inhale

Make Words: Tell children how many letters to use to make each word. (A slash in the Make Words list indicates that words can be made with the same letters. An underline __ in the letter bank or on the letter strip indicates that a blank space is needed for the secret place.)

Emphasize how changing just one letter or rearranging letters makes different words:

"Change 1 letter in **gave** to spell **save**."

"Use the same letters in **save** to spell **vase**."

When children are not just adding or changing one letter, cue them to start over.

"Start over and use 5 new letters to spell **glass**."

Give meaning or sentence clues when needed to clarify the word they are making:

"Use 6 letters to spell **savage**. The dogs ran in a pack like wolves and were fierce and **savage**."

Give children one minute to figure out the secret place and then give clues if needed.

"Our secret place is the name of a city in Nevada with two words in its name."

Sort Rhymes

Reading Transfer: "Pretend you are reading and come to a new word." Have children put the words under the appropriate rhymes and use the rhymes to decode them.

Spelling Transfer: "Pretend you are writing and need to spell these words." Have children tell you how the words begin. Then, have children find and use the appropriate rhymes to finish spelling the new words.

Step-by-step directions for a sample *Making Places* lesson are on pages 9–13.

Liberia

a e i i b l r

Make Words: Tell children how many letters to use to make each word. (A slash in the Make Words list indicates that words can be made with the same letters. An underline __ in the letter bank or on the letter strip indicates that a blank space is needed for the secret place.)

Emphasize how changing just one letter or rearranging letters makes different words:

"Add a letter to **bar** to spell **bare**. When the leaves fell, all of the trees were **bare**."

"Change 1 letter in **bail** to spell **rail**."

"Use the same letters in **able** to spell **bale**."

When children are not just adding or changing one letter, cue them to start over.

"Start over and use 4 new letters to spell **able**."

Give meaning or sentence clues when needed to clarify the word they are making:

"Use the same letters in **bare** to spell another kind of **bear**. A big brown **bear** came to our campsite."

Always alert children when they are making a name and expect them to use a capital letter.

"Change 1 letter and spell the name **Lib**."

Give children one minute to figure out the secret place and then give clues if needed.

"Our secret place is a country in Africa that begins with **L**."

Sort Homophones

Sort Rhymes

Reading Transfer: "Pretend you are reading and come to a new word." Have children put the words under the appropriate rhymes and use the rhymes to decode them.

Spelling Transfer: "Pretend you are writing and need to spell these words." Have children tell you how the words begin. Then, have children find and use the appropriate rhymes to finish spelling the new words.

Step-by-step directions for a sample *Making Places* lesson are on pages 9–13.

MAKE WORDS

lab
Lib
rib
bar
bare/bear
able/bale
bail
rail
Liberia

SORT WORDS

Homophones:
bare, bear; bale, bail

Rhymes:
Lib   bail
rib   rail

TRANSFER WORDS

Reading:
toenail   derail

Spelling:
blackmail   detail

Little Rock

e i o c k l l r t t _

MAKE WORDS

rock
lock
locker
locket
rocket
recoil
little
ticket
ticker
tickle
trickle
Little Rock

SORT WORDS

Related Words:
lock, locker, locket

Rhymes:
tickle   rock   locket
trickle lock   rocket

TRANSFER WORDS

Reading:
pocket livestock

Spelling:
socket pickle

Make Words: Tell children how many letters to use to make each word. (A slash in the Make Words list indicates that words can be made with the same letters. An underline __ in the letter bank or on the letter strip indicates that a blank space is needed for the secret place.)

Emphasize how changing just one letter or rearranging letters makes different words:

> "Add 2 letters to **lock** to spell **locker**."

> "Change 1 letter in **locker** to spell **locket**."

When children are not just adding or changing one letter, cue them to start over.

> "Start over and use 6 new letters to spell **ticket**."

Give meaning or sentence clues when needed to clarify the word they are making:

> "Add 1 letter to spell **trickle**. We sat and watched the water **trickle** down from the mountains into the stream."

Give children one minute to figure out the secret place and then give clues if needed.

> "Our secret place is the name of a city in Arkansas with two words in its name, and we made both the words."

Sort Related Words

Sort Rhymes

Reading Transfer: "Pretend you are reading and come to a new word." Have children put the words under the appropriate rhymes and use the rhymes to decode them.

Spelling Transfer: "Pretend you are writing and need to spell these words." Have children tell you how the words begin. Then, have children find and use the appropriate rhymes to finish spelling the new words.

Step-by-step directions for a sample *Making Places* lesson are on pages 9–13.

Making Places • CD-104108 • © Carson-Dellosa

London, England

a e o o d d g l l n n n n , _

Make Words: Tell children how many letters to use to make each word. (A slash in the Make Words list indicates that words can be made with the same letters. An underline __ in the letter bank or on the letter strip indicates that a blank space is needed for the secret place.)

Emphasize how changing just one letter or rearranging letters makes different words:

> "Add a letter to **angle** to spell **dangle**."

> "Change 1 letter in **dodge** to spell **lodge**."

> "Use the same letters in **angel** to spell **angle**."

When children are not just adding or changing one letter, cue them to start over.

> "Start over and use 6 letters to spell **golden**."

Give meaning or sentence clues when needed to clarify the word they are making:

> "Use 6 letters to spell **gallon**. We bought a **gallon** of milk."

Always alert children when they are making a name and expect them to use a capital letter.

> "Use 6 letters and spell the city of **London**."

Give children one minute to figure out the secret place and then give clues if needed.

> "Our secret place is a capital and a country, and we spelled the capital."

Sort Related Words

Sort Rhymes

Reading Transfer: "Pretend you are reading and come to a new word." Have children put the words under the appropriate rhymes and use the rhymes to decode them.

Spelling Transfer: "Pretend you are writing and need to spell these words." Have children tell you how the words begin. Then, have children find and use the appropriate rhymes to finish spelling the new words.

Step-by-step directions for a sample *Making Places* lesson are on pages 9–13.

MAKE WORDS

old
gold
dodge
lodge
angel/angle
dangle
London
golden
gallon
London, England

SORT WORDS

Related Words:
gold, golden

Rhymes:

old	dodge	angle
gold	lodge	dangle

TRANSFER WORDS

Reading:
stronghold   withhold

Spelling:
retold   tangle

Los Angeles

a e e o g l l n s s __

MAKE WORDS

go
goes
long
song
lane
sane
legs
logs
Laos
angle/angel
season
slogan
gallons
Los Angeles

SORT WORDS

Related Words:
go, goes

Rhymes:
long   lane
song   sane

TRANSFER WORDS

Reading:
prolong   insane

Spelling:
belong   along

Make Words: Tell children how many letters to use to make each word. (A slash in the Make Words list indicates that words can be made with the same letters. An underline __ in the letter bank or on the letter strip indicates that a blank space is needed for the secret place.)

Emphasize how changing just one letter or rearranging letters makes different words:

"Add 2 letters to **go** to spell **goes**."

"Change 1 letter in **legs** to spell **logs**."

"Use the same letters in **angle** to spell **angel**."

When children are not just adding or changing one letter, cue them to start over.

"Start over and use 7 new letters to spell **gallons**."

Give meaning or sentence clues when needed to clarify the word they are making:

"Use 6 letters to spell **slogan**. My sister was running for class president and needed a good campaign **slogan**."

Always alert children when they are making a name and expect them to use a capital letter.

"Take 4 letters and spell the country of **Laos**."

Give children one minute to figure out the secret place and then give clues if needed.

"Our secret place is the name of a city in California with two words in its name."

Sort Related Words

Sort Rhymes

Reading Transfer: "Pretend you are reading and come to a new word." Have children put the words under the appropriate rhymes and use the rhymes to decode them.

Spelling Transfer: "Pretend you are writing and need to spell these words." Have children tell you how the words begin. Then, have children find and use the appropriate rhymes to finish spelling the new words.

Step-by-step directions for a sample *Making Places* lesson are on pages 9–13.

Louisiana

Make Words: Tell children how many letters to use to make each word. (A slash in the Make Words list indicates that words can be made with the same letters. An underline __ in the letter bank or on the letter strip indicates that a blank space is needed for the secret place.)

Emphasize how changing just one letter or rearranging letters makes different words:

"Add a letter to **ail** to spell **sail**."

"Change 1 letter in **sail** to spell **soil**."

"Use the same letters in **nails** to spell **snail**."

When children are not just adding or changing one letter, cue them to start over.

"Start over and use 5 new letters to spell **lions**."

Give meaning or sentence clues when needed to clarify the word they are making:

"Start over and use 5 letters to spell **alias**. The movie star did not want to be recognized, so he registered at the hotel using an **alias**."

Always alert children when they are making a name and expect them to use a capital letter.

"Take 4 letters and spell the continent of **Asia**."

Give children one minute to figure out the secret place and then give clues if needed.

"Our secret place is the name of a state that starts with **L**."

Sort Homophones

Sort Rhymes

Reading Transfer: "Pretend you are reading and come to a new word." Have children put the words under the appropriate rhymes and use the rhymes to decode them.

Spelling Transfer: "Pretend you are writing and need to spell these words." Have children tell you how the words begin. Then, have children find and use the appropriate rhymes to finish spelling the new words.

Step-by-step directions for a sample *Making Places* lesson are on pages 9–13.

MAKE WORDS

sun
son
oil
ail
sail
soil
lions
also/Laos
Asia
nail
nails/snail
alias
Louis
Louisiana

SORT WORDS

Homophones:
sun, son

Rhymes:
ail   oil
sail   soil
nail
snail

TRANSFER WORDS

Reading:
prevail   turmoil

Spelling:
detail   recoil

Madrid, Spain

aaiiddmnprs, __

MAKE WORDS

Pam
spam
rain
India
Paris
panda
rapid
Spain
sprain
marina
Parisian
Madrid, Spain

SORT WORDS

Related Words:
Paris, Parisian

Rhymes:
rain   Pam
Spain   spam
sprain

TRANSFER WORDS

Reading:
milligram   telegram

Spelling:
exam   program

Make Words: Tell children how many letters to use to make each word. (A slash in the Make Words list indicates that words can be made with the same letters. An underline __ in the letter bank or on the letter strip indicates that a blank space is needed for the secret place.)

Emphasize how changing just one letter or rearranging letters makes different words:

"Add a letter to **Pam** to spell **spam**."

When children are not just adding or changing one letter, cue them to start over.

"Start over and use 6 new letters to spell **marina**."

Give meaning or sentence clues when needed to clarify the word they are making:

"Start over and use 8 letters to spell **Parisian**. A **Parisian** is a person who lives in Paris."

Always alert children when they are making a name and expect them to use a capital letter.

"Take 5 letters and spell the city of **Paris**. **Paris** is the capital of France."

Give children one minute to figure out the secret place and then give clues if needed.

"Our secret place is a capital and country, and we made the name of the country."

Sort Related Words

Sort Rhymes

Reading Transfer: "Pretend you are reading and come to a new word." Have children put the words under the appropriate rhymes and use the rhymes to decode them.

Spelling Transfer: "Pretend you are writing and need to spell these words." Have children tell you how the words begin. Then, have children find and use the appropriate rhymes to finish spelling the new words.

Step-by-step directions for a sample *Making Places* lesson are on pages 9–13.

Manitoba

a a i o b m n t

Make Words: Tell children how many letters to use to make each word. (A slash in the Make Words list indicates that words can be made with the same letters. An underline __ in the letter bank or on the letter strip indicates that a blank space is needed for the secret place.)

Emphasize how changing just one letter or rearranging letters makes different words:

> "Add a letter to **mat** to spell **moat**."

> "Change 1 letter in **moat** to spell **boat**."

When children are not just adding or changing one letter, cue them to start over.

> "Start over and use 4 new letters to spell **tomb**."

Give meaning or sentence clues when needed to clarify the word they are making:

> "Start over and use 6 letters to spell **obtain.** I went to the embassy to **obtain** a visa to go to China."

Always alert children when they are making a name and expect them to use a capital letter.

> "Start over and use 6 letters to spell **Batman®**."

Give children one minute to figure out the secret place and then give clues if needed.

> "Our secret place is a province in Canada that begins with an **M**."

Sort Related Words

Sort Rhymes

Reading Transfer: "Pretend you are reading and come to a new word." Have children put the words under the appropriate rhymes and use the rhymes to decode them.

Spelling Transfer: "Pretend you are writing and need to spell these words." Have children tell you how the words begin. Then, have children find and use the appropriate rhymes to finish spelling the new words.

Step-by-step directions for a sample *Making Places* lesson are on pages 9–13.

MAKE WORDS

bat
mat
moat
boat
bait
tomb
omit
mania
obtain
Batman®
boatman
Manitoba

SORT WORDS

Related Words:
bat, Batman®; boat, boatman

Rhymes:
bat	boat
mat	moat

TRANSFER WORDS

Reading:
lifeboat   raincoat

Spelling:
afloat   sailboat

Maryland

a a d l m n r y

MAKE WORDS

mad
lad
Amy
any
many
Mary/army
yard
yarn
darn
Dylan
alarm
madly
Maryland

SORT WORDS

Related Words:
mad, madly

Rhymes:
mad   yarn   any
lad   darn   many

TRANSFER WORDS

Reading:
undergrad   nomad
Spelling:
granddad   Chad

Make Words: Tell children how many letters to use to make each word. (A slash in the Make Words list indicates that words can be made with the same letters. An underline __ in the letter bank or on the letter strip indicates that a blank space is needed for the secret place.)

Emphasize how changing just one letter or rearranging letters makes different words:

"Add a letter to **any** to spell **many**."

"Change 1 letter in **yard** to spell **yarn**."

"Use the same letters in **Mary** to spell **army**."

When children are not just adding or changing one letter, cue them to start over.

"Start over and use 5 new letters to spell **alarm**."

Give meaning or sentence clues when needed to clarify the word they are making:

"Start over and use 5 letters to spell **madly**. The newlyweds were **madly** in love."

Always alert children when they are making a name and expect them to use a capital letter.

"Take 5 letters and spell the name **Dylan**."

Give children one minute to figure out the secret place and then give clues if needed.

"Our secret place is the name of a state that starts with **M**."

Sort Related Words

Sort Rhymes

Reading Transfer: "Pretend you are reading and come to a new word." Have children put the words under the appropriate rhymes and use the rhymes to decode them.

Spelling Transfer: "Pretend you are writing and need to spell these words." Have children tell you how the words begin. Then, have children find and use the appropriate rhymes to finish spelling the new words.

Step-by-step directions for a sample *Making Places* lesson are on pages 9–13.

Massachusetts

a a e u c h m s s s s t t

Make Words: Tell children how many letters to use to make each word. (A slash in the Make Words list indicates that words can be made with the same letters. An underline __ in the letter bank or on the letter strip indicates that a blank space is needed for the secret place.)

Emphasize how changing just one letter or rearranging letters makes different words:

"Add a letter to **each** to spell **teach**."

"Change 1 letter in **cashes** to spell **mashes**."

"Use the same letters in **teach** to spell **cheat**."

When children are not just adding or changing one letter, cue them to start over.

"Start over and use 5 new letters to spell **smash**."

Give meaning or sentence clues when needed to clarify the word they are making:

"Start over and use 6 letters to spell **attach**. We used tape to **attach** the decorations to the wall."

Give children one minute to figure out the secret place and then give clues if needed.

"Our secret place is the name of a state that starts with **M**."

Sort Related Words and point out that instead of adding **s** to words that end in **sh** or **ch,** you add **es.**

Sort Rhymes

Reading Transfer: "Pretend you are reading and come to a new word." Have children put the words under the appropriate rhymes and use the rhymes to decode them.

Spelling Transfer: "Pretend you are writing and need to spell these words." Have children tell you how the words begin. Then, have children find and use the appropriate rhymes to finish spelling the new words.

Step-by-step directions for a sample *Making Places* lesson are on pages 9–13.

MAKE WORDS

cute
mute
cash
mash
each
teach/cheat
smash
match
attach
cashes
mashes
matches
attaches
Massachusetts

SORT WORDS

Related Words:
cash, cashes; mash, mashes;
match, matches;
attach, attaches

Rhymes:
cash   cashes   each   cute
mash   mashes   teach   mute
smash

TRANSFER WORDS

Reading:
commute   pollute

Spelling:
compute   salute

Mexico City

eiiocc m t x y __

MAKE WORDS

it
ice
mice
time
exit
city
come
comet
comic
toxic
exotic
Mexico
Mexico City

SORT WORDS

Rhymes:
ice
mice

TRANSFER WORDS

Reading:
entice   slice

Spelling:
spice   advice

Make Words: Tell children how many letters to use to make each word. (A slash in the Make Words list indicates that words can be made with the same letters. An underline __ in the letter bank or on the letter strip indicates that a blank space is needed for the secret place.)

Emphasize how changing just one letter or rearranging letters makes different words:

"Add a letter to **ice** to spell **mice**."

"Change 2 letters in **comet** to spell **comic**."

When children are not just adding or changing one letter, cue them to start over.

"Start over and use 6 letters to spell **exotic**."

Give meaning or sentence clues when needed to clarify the word they are making:

"Use 5 letters to spell **toxic**. After the spill, the water in the stream was **toxic** to the fish."

Always alert children when they are making a name and expect them to use a capital letter.

"Start over and use 6 new letters to spell the country of **Mexico**."

Give children one minute to figure out the secret place and then give clues if needed.

"Our secret place is the capital of Mexico."

Sort Rhymes

Reading Transfer: "Pretend you are reading and come to a new word." Have children put the words under the appropriate rhymes and use the rhymes to decode them.

Spelling Transfer: "Pretend you are writing and need to spell these words." Have children tell you how the words begin. Then, have children find and use the appropriate rhymes to finish spelling the new words.

Step-by-step directions for a sample *Making Places* lesson are on pages 9–13.

Michigan

Make Words: Tell children how many letters to use to make each word. (A slash in the Make Words list indicates that words can be made with the same letters. An underline __ in the letter bank or on the letter strip indicates that a blank space is needed for the secret place.)

Emphasize how changing just one letter or rearranging letters makes different words:

> "Change 1 letter in **main** to spell **gain**."

> "Use the same letters in **chin** to spell **inch**."

When children are not just adding or changing one letter, cue them to start over.

> "Start over and use 5 new letters to spell **magic**."

Give meaning or sentence clues when needed to clarify the word they are making:

> "Start over and use 3 letters to spell **nag**. Do your parents have to **nag** you to do your homework?"

Always alert children when they are making a name and expect them to use a capital letter.

> "Use the same letters and spell the country of **China**."

Give children one minute to figure out the secret place and then give clues if needed.

> "Our secret place is the name of a state that starts with **M**."

Sort Related Words

Sort Rhymes

Reading Transfer: "Pretend you are reading and come to a new word." Have children put the words under the appropriate rhymes and use the rhymes to decode them.

Spelling Transfer: "Pretend you are writing and need to spell these words." Have children tell you how the words begin. Then, have children find and use the appropriate rhymes to finish spelling the new words.

Step-by-step directions for a sample *Making Places* lesson are on pages 9–13.

MAKE WORDS

in
can
man
nag
hag
aim
chin/inch
main
gain
chain/China
magic
aiming
Michigan

SORT WORDS

Related Words:
aim, aiming

Rhymes:

nag	main	can
hag	gain	man
	chain	

TRANSFER WORDS

Reading:
beanbag   restrain

Spelling:
complain   explain

Minneapolis

MAKE WORDS

sane
line
mine
mile
smile
Maine
insane
simple
sample
aliens
mansion
pension
Minneapolis

SORT WORDS

Words Ending in sion:
mansion, pension

Related Words:
sane, insane

Rhymes:
line   mile
mine   smile

TRANSFER WORDS

Reading:
reptile   decline

Spelling:
define   exile

Make Words: Tell children how many letters to use to make each word. (A slash in the Make Words list indicates that words can be made with the same letters. An underline __ in the letter bank or on the letter strip indicates that a blank space is needed for the secret place.)

Emphasize how changing just one letter or rearranging letters makes different words:

"Add a letter to **mile** to spell **smile**."

"Change 1 letter in **simple** to spell **sample**."

When children are not just adding or changing one letter, cue them to start over.

"Start over and use 6 new letters to spell **simple**."

Give meaning or sentence clues when needed to clarify the word they are making:

"Start over and use 7 letters to spell **pension**. My grandma is retired and gets a **pension** check from the company she worked for."

Always alert children when they are making a name and expect them to use a capital letter.

"Start over and use 5 new letters to spell the state of **Maine**."

Give children one minute to figure out the secret place and then give clues if needed.

"Our secret place is a city in Minnesota that begins with **M**."

Sort Words Ending in sion

Sort Related Words

Sort Rhymes

Reading Transfer: "Pretend you are reading and come to a new word." Have children put the words under the appropriate rhymes and use the rhymes to decode them.

Spelling Transfer: "Pretend you are writing and need to spell these words." Have children tell you how the words begin. Then, have children find and use the appropriate rhymes to finish spelling the new words.

Step-by-step directions for a sample *Making Places* lesson are on pages 9–13.

Minnesota

a e i o m n n s t

Make Words: Tell children how many letters to use to make each word. (A slash in the Make Words list indicates that words can be made with the same letters. An underline ___ in the letter bank or on the letter strip indicates that a blank space is needed for the secret place.)

Emphasize how changing just one letter or rearranging letters makes different words:

> "Change 1 letter in **meat** to spell **seat**."

> "Use the same letters in **mean** to spell **name**."

When children are not just adding or changing one letter, cue them to start over.

> "Start over and use 5 new letters to spell **moist**."

Give meaning or sentence clues when needed to clarify the word they are making:

> "Start over and use 7 letters to spell **tension**. During the tug-of-war, there was so much **tension** on the rope that it broke."

Always alert children when they are making a name and expect them to use a capital letter.

> "Start over and use 5 letters to spell the state of **Maine**."

Give children one minute to figure out the secret place and then give clues if needed.

> "Our secret place is the name of a state that starts with **M**."

Sort Words Ending in sion and tion and talk about how this final syllable sounds the same but can be spelled in these two ways.

Sort Related Words

Sort Rhymes

Reading Transfer: "Pretend you are reading and come to a new word." Have children put the words under the appropriate rhymes and use the rhymes to decode them.

Spelling Transfer: "Pretend you are writing and need to spell these words." Have children tell you how the words begin. Then, have children find and use the appropriate rhymes to finish spelling the new words.

Step-by-step directions for a sample *Making Places* lesson are on pages 9–13.

MAKE WORDS

mean/name
tame/team/mate/meat
seat
steam
moist
Maine
nation
mention
tension
mansion
moisten
Minnesota

SORT WORDS

Words Ending in sion and tion:
tension, mansion;
nation, mention

Related Words:
moist, moisten

Rhymes:
name   team   meat
tame   steam   seat

TRANSFER WORDS

Reading:
nickname   mainstream

Spelling:
downstream   aflame

Montana

MAKE WORDS

at
an
ant/tan
man
mat
oat
not
Tom
moan
moat/atom
Anna
Montana

SORT WORDS

Rhymes:

at	oat	an
mat	moat	tan
		man

TRANSFER WORDS

Reading:
scapegoat acrobat

Spelling:
combat lifeboat

Make Words: Tell children how many letters to use to make each word. (A slash in the Make Words list indicates that words can be made with the same letters. An underline __ in the letter bank or on the letter strip indicates that a blank space is needed for the secret place.)

Emphasize how changing just one letter or rearranging letters makes different words:

"Add a letter to **an** to spell **ant**."

"Change 1 letter in **mat** to spell **oat**."

"Use the same letters in **moat** to spell **atom**."

When children are not just adding or changing one letter, cue them to start over.

"Start over and use 4 new letters to spell the name **Anna**."

Give meaning or sentence clues when needed to clarify the word they are making:

"Change 1 letter to spell **moat**. They crossed the drawbridge over the **moat** to enter the castle."

Always alert children when they are making a name and expect them to use a capital letter.

"Take 3 letters and spell the name **Tom**."

Give children one minute to figure out the secret place and then give clues if needed.

"Our secret place is the name of a state that starts with **M**."

Sort Rhymes

Reading Transfer: "Pretend you are reading and come to a new word." Have children put the words under the appropriate rhymes and use the rhymes to decode them.

Spelling Transfer: "Pretend you are writing and need to spell these words." Have children tell you how the words begin. Then, have children find and use the appropriate rhymes to finish spelling the new words.

Step-by-step directions for a sample *Making Places* lesson are on pages 9–13.

Montgomery

e o o g m m n r t y

Make Words: Tell children how many letters to use to make each word. (A slash in the Make Words list indicates that words can be made with the same letters. An underline __ in the letter bank or on the letter strip indicates that a blank space is needed for the secret place.)

Emphasize how changing just one letter or rearranging letters makes different words:

> "Add a letter to **room** to spell **roomy**."

> "Change 1 letter in **more** to spell **tore**."

> "Use the same letters in **Rome** to spell **more**."

When children are not just adding or changing one letter, cue them to start over.

> "Start over and use 5 new letters to spell **money**."

Give meaning or sentence clues when needed to clarify the word they are making:

> "Use 5 letters to spell **groom**. Both the bride and the **groom** looked incredibly happy."

Always alert children when they are making a name and expect them to use a capital letter.

> "Add 1 letter and spell the name **Troy**."

Give children one minute to figure out the secret place and then give clues if needed.

> "Our secret place is the capital of Alabama and begins with **M**."

Sort Related Words

Sort Rhymes

Reading Transfer: "Pretend you are reading and come to a new word." Have children put the words under the appropriate rhymes and use the rhymes to decode them.

Spelling Transfer: "Pretend you are writing and need to spell these words." Have children tell you how the words begin. Then, have children find and use the appropriate rhymes to finish spelling the new words.

Step-by-step directions for a sample *Making Places* lesson are on pages 9–13.

MAKE WORDS

Roy
Troy
Rome/more
tore
memo
room
roomy
groom
money
motor
memory
moment
Oregon
Montgomery

SORT WORDS

Related Words:
room, roomy

Rhymes:
| more | room | Roy |
| tore | groom | Troy |

TRANSFER WORDS

Reading:
annoy   destroy

Spelling:
enjoy   employ

Montreal

MAKE WORDS

name
lame/male
tale
tame/team
rent
Rome
lemon/melon
metal
mental
normal
rental
Montreal

SORT WORDS

Words Ending in al:
metal, mental, normal, rental, Montreal

Related Words:
rent, rental

Rhymes:
name   male   mental
lame   tale   rental
tame

TRANSFER WORDS

Reading:
nickname   wholesale

Spelling:
central   became

Make Words: Tell children how many letters to use to make each word. (A slash in the Make Words list indicates that words can be made with the same letters. An underline __ in the letter bank or on the letter strip indicates that a blank space is needed for the secret place.)

Emphasize how changing just one letter or rearranging letters makes different words:

"Add a letter to **metal** to spell **mental**."

"Change 1 letter in **tale** to spell **tame**."

"Use the same letters in **lemon** to spell **melon**."

When children are not just adding or changing one letter, cue them to start over.

"Start over and use 6 new letters to spell **normal**."

Give meaning or sentence clues when needed to clarify the word they are making:

"Start over and use 6 new letters to spell **rental**. The landlord owned several **rental** houses."

Always alert children when they are making a name and expect them to use a capital letter.

"Start over and use 4 letters to spell the city of **Rome**. **Rome** is the capital of Italy."

Give children one minute to figure out the secret place and then give clues if needed.

"Our secret place is a big city in Canada."

Sort Words Ending in al

Sort Related Words

Sort Rhymes

Reading Transfer: "Pretend you are reading and come to a new word." Have children put the words under the appropriate rhymes and use the rhymes to decode them.

Spelling Transfer: "Pretend you are writing and need to spell these words." Have children tell you how the words begin. Then, have children find and use the appropriate rhymes to finish spelling the new words.

Step-by-step directions for a sample *Making Places* lesson are on pages 9–13.

Moscow, Russia

a i o o u c m r s s s w , __

Make Words: Tell children how many letters to use to make each word. (A slash in the Make Words list indicates that words can be made with the same letters. An underline __ in the letter bank or on the letter strip indicates that a blank space is needed for the secret place.)

Emphasize how changing just one letter or rearranging letters makes different words:

> "Add a letter to **cross** to spell **across**."

> "Change a letter in **warms** to spell **worms**."

When children are not just adding or changing one letter, cue them to start over.

> "Start over and use 5 new letters to spell **cross**."

Give meaning or sentence clues when needed to clarify the word they are making:

> "Start over and use 5 letters to spell **Cairo**. **Cairo** is the capital of Egypt."

Always alert children when they are making a name and expect them to use a capital letter.

> "Take 5 letters and spell the name **Oscar**."

Give children one minute to figure out the secret place and then give clues if needed.

> "Our secret place is a capital and country, and we made one of the words."

Sort Related Words

Sort Rhymes

Reading Transfer: "Pretend you are reading and come to a new word." Have children put the words under the appropriate rhymes and use the rhymes to decode them.

Spelling Transfer: "Pretend you are writing and need to spell these words." Have children tell you how the words begin. Then, have children find and use the appropriate rhymes to finish spelling the new words.

Step-by-step directions for a sample *Making Places* lesson are on pages 9–13.

MAKE WORDS

ram
moss
Iowa
scram
warms
worms
Oscar
music
Cairo
cross
across
Russia
osmosis
Moscow, Russia

SORT WORDS

Related Words:
cross, across

Rhymes:
ram	moss
scram	cross
	across

TRANSFER WORDS

Reading:
diagram   program

Spelling:
exam   floss

mountains

MAKE WORDS

at
man
tan/Nat
sat
tuna/aunt
noun
union
amount
nation
mansion
mountains

SORT WORDS

Rhymes:
man   at
tan   sat

TRANSFER WORDS

Reading:
caravan   wildcat
Spelling:
dishpan   combat

Make Words: Tell children how many letters to use to make each word. (A slash in the Make Words list indicates that words can be made with the same letters. An underline __ in the letter bank or on the letter strip indicates that a blank space is needed for the secret place.)

Emphasize how changing just one letter or rearranging letters makes different words:

"Change 1 letter in **man** to spell **tan**."

"Use the same letters in **tuna** to spell **aunt**."

When children are not just adding or changing one letter, cue them to start over.

"Start over and use 7 new letters to spell **mansion**."

Give meaning or sentence clues when needed to clarify the word they are making:

"Start over and use 5 letters to spell **union**. The **union** workers are on strike."

Always alert children when they are making a name and expect them to use a capital letter.

"Use the same letters in **tan** to spell the name **Nat**."

Give children one minute to figure out the secret place and then give clues if needed.

"Our secret place is not a specific place this time and does not start with a capital letter. It is where many people go to ski or hike."

Sort Rhymes

Reading Transfer: "Pretend you are reading and come to a new word." Have children put the words under the appropriate rhymes and use the rhymes to decode them.

Spelling Transfer: "Pretend you are writing and need to spell these words." Have children tell you how the words begin. Then, have children find and use the appropriate rhymes to finish spelling the new words.

Step-by-step directions for a sample *Making Places* lesson are on pages 9–13.

Nashville

a e i h l l n s v

Make Words: Tell children how many letters to use to make each word. (A slash in the Make Words list indicates that words can be made with the same letters. An underline __ in the letter bank or on the letter strip indicates that a blank space is needed for the secret place.)

Emphasize how changing just one letter or rearranging letters makes different words:

> "Add a letter to **save** to spell **slave**."

> "Change 1 letter in **slave** to spell **shave**."

When children are not just adding or changing one letter, cue them to start over.

> "Start over and use 5 new letters to spell **alive**."

Give meaning or sentence clues when needed to clarify the word they are making:

> "Use 4 letters to spell another **sale**. There is a big **sale** at Wal-Mart®."

Give children one minute to figure out the secret place and then give clues if needed.

> "Our secret place is the capital of Tennessee, and it begins with **N**."

Sort Homophones

Sort Related Words

Sort Rhymes

Reading Transfer: "Pretend you are reading and come to a new word." Have children put the words under the appropriate rhymes and use the rhymes to decode them.

Spelling Transfer: "Pretend you are writing and need to spell these words." Have children tell you how the words begin. Then, have children find and use the appropriate rhymes to finish spelling the new words.

Step-by-step directions for a sample *Making Places* lesson are on pages 9–13.

MAKE WORDS

live
line
vine
sell
sail
sale
save
slave
shave
shine
shell
alive
shaven
Nashville

SORT WORDS

Homophones:
sail, sale

Related Words:
live, alive; shave, shaven

Rhymes:
line	save	sell
vine	slave	shell
shine		

TRANSFER WORDS

Reading:
farewell   engrave

Spelling:
misspell   behave

nations

a i o n n s t

MAKE WORDS

in
inn
tan
ton
son
into
ants/Stan
stain/saint/satin
nations

SORT WORDS

Related Words:
in, into

Rhymes:
ton   tan
son   Stan

TRANSFER WORDS

Reading:
Superman®   caravan

Spelling:
dishpan   began

Make Words: Tell children how many letters to use to make each word. (A slash in the Make Words list indicates that words can be made with the same letters. An underline __ in the letter bank or on the letter strip indicates that a blank space is needed for the secret place.)

Emphasize how changing just one letter or rearranging letters makes different words:

"Change 1 letter in **ton** to spell **son**."

"Use the same letters in **stain** to spell **saint**. Use these letters again to spell **satin**."

When children are not just adding or changing one letter, cue them to start over.

"Start over and use 4 new letters to spell **into**."

Give meaning or sentence clues when needed to clarify the word they are making:

"Add a letter to **in** to spell another kind of **inn**. We went on vacation and stayed at the a little country inn."

Always alert children when they are making a name and expect them to use a capital letter.

"Use the same letters and spell the name **Stan**."

Give children one minute to figure out the secret place and then give clues if needed.

"Our secret place is another word for countries that starts with **n**."

Sort Related Words

Sort Rhymes

Reading Transfer: "Pretend you are reading and come to a new word." Have children put the words under the appropriate rhymes and use the rhymes to decode them.

Spelling Transfer: "Pretend you are writing and need to spell these words." Have children tell you how the words begin. Then, have children find and use the appropriate rhymes to finish spelling the new words.

Step-by-step directions for a sample *Making Places* lesson are on pages 9–13.

Nebraska

a a e b k n r s

Make Words: Tell children how many letters to use to make each word. (A slash in the Make Words list indicates that words can be made with the same letters. An underline __ in the letter bank or on the letter strip indicates that a blank space is needed for the secret place.)

Emphasize how changing just one letter or rearranging letters makes different words:

> "Add a letter to **bakers** to spell **bankers**."

> "Change 1 letter in **rank** to spell **sank**."

> "Use the same letters in **bake** to spell **beak**."

When children are not just adding or changing one letter, cue them to start over.

> "Start over and use 6 new letters to spell **bakers**."

Give meaning or sentence clues when needed to clarify the word they are making:

> "Add 1 letter to spell **bask**. Sunbathers **bask** in the sun."

Always alert children when they are making a name and expect them to use a capital letter.

> "Use 5 letters to spell **Arabs**. Some people who live in the Middle East are **Arabs**."

Give children one minute to figure out the secret place and then give clues if needed.

> "Our secret place is the name of a state that starts with **N**."

Sort Related Words

Sort Rhymes

Reading Transfer: "Pretend you are reading and come to a new word." Have children put the words under the appropriate rhymes and use the rhymes to decode them.

Spelling Transfer: "Pretend you are writing and need to spell these words." Have children tell you how the words begin. Then, have children find and use the appropriate rhymes to finish spelling the new words.

Step-by-step directions for a sample *Making Places* lesson are on pages 9–13.

MAKE WORDS

ask
bask
bank
rank
sank
rake
bake/beak
sneak/snake
Karen
Arabs
bakers
bankers
Nebraska

SORT WORDS

Related Words:
bake, bakers; bank, bankers

Rhymes:

ask	bake	beak	bank
bask	rake	sneak	rank
	snake		sank

TRANSFER WORDS

Reading:
mistake   cupcake

Spelling:
pancake   awake

New Brunswick

MAKE WORDS

win
rise
wise
wire
wick
sick
bike
biker
brick
unwise
winners
New Brunswick

SORT WORDS

Related Words:
win, winners; wise, unwise;
bike, biker

Rhymes:
wise	wick
rise	sick
unwise	brick

TRANSFER WORDS

Reading:
revise   surprise

Spelling:
advise   slick

Make Words: Tell children how many letters to use to make each word. (A slash in the Make Words list indicates that words can be made with the same letters. An underline __ in the letter bank or on the letter strip indicates that a blank space is needed for the secret place.)

Emphasize how changing just one letter or rearranging letters makes different words:

"Add a letter to **bike** to spell **biker**."

"Change 1 letter in **wise** to spell **wire**."

When children are not just adding or changing one letter, cue them to start over.

"Start over and use 6 new letters to spell **unwise**."

Give meaning or sentence clues when needed to clarify the word they are making:

"Use 4 letters to spell **wick**. The part of the candle you light is called the **wick**."

Give children one minute to figure out the secret place and then give clues if needed.

"Our secret place is a province in Canada, and the two words begin with **N** and **B**."

Sort Related Words

Sort Rhymes

Reading Transfer: "Pretend you are reading and come to a new word." Have children put the words under the appropriate rhymes and use the rhymes to decode them.

Spelling Transfer: "Pretend you are writing and need to spell these words." Have children tell you how the words begin. Then, have children find and use the appropriate rhymes to finish spelling the new words.

Step-by-step directions for a sample *Making Places* lesson are on pages 9–13.

Newfoundland

a e o u d d f l n n w

Make Words: Tell children how many letters to use to make each word. (A slash in the Make Words list indicates that words can be made with the same letters. An underline __ in the letter bank or on the letter strip indicates that a blank space is needed for the secret place.)

Emphasize how changing just one letter or rearranging letters makes different words:

"Add a letter to **law** to spell **flaw**."

"Change 1 letter in **lawn** to spell **dawn**."

When children are not just adding or changing one letter, cue them to start over.

"Start over and use 4 new letters to spell **fold**."

Give meaning or sentence clues when needed to clarify the word they are making:

"Start over and use 7 letters to spell **wounded**. The **wounded** soldiers were flown to the hospital in Germany."

Give children one minute to figure out the secret place and then give clues if needed.

"Our secret place is a province in Canada that begins with **N**."

Sort Related Words

Sort Rhymes

Reading Transfer: "Pretend you are reading and come to a new word." Have children put the words under the appropriate rhymes and use the rhymes to decode them.

Spelling Transfer: "Pretend you are writing and need to spell these words." Have children tell you how the words begin. Then, have children find and use the appropriate rhymes to finish spelling the new words.

Step-by-step directions for a sample *Making Places* lesson are on pages 9–13.

MAKE WORDS

old
new
few
law
flaw
lawn
dawn
fold
load
unfold
unload
wounded
Newfoundland

SORT WORDS

Related Words:
fold, unfold; load, unload

Rhymes:

new	law	old	lawn
few	flaw	fold	dawn
			unfold

TRANSFER WORDS

Reading:
withdrew   curfew

Spelling:
withdraw   withdrawn

New Hampshire

MAKE WORDS

new
ape
rap
wrap
name
harp
sharp
shape
Paris
Maine
phase
phrase
nephew
rename
reshape
sharpen
New Hampshire

SORT WORDS

Ph Words:
nephew, phase, phrase

Related Words:
sharp, sharpen; name, rename;
shape, reshape

Rhymes:
sharp   ape
harp   shape
         reshape

TRANSFER WORDS

Reading:
escape   shipshape

Spelling:
landscape   seascape

Make Words: Tell children how many letters to use to make each word. (A slash in the Make Words list indicates that words can be made with the same letters. An underline __ in the letter bank or on the letter strip indicates that a blank space is needed for the secret place.)

Emphasize how changing just one letter or rearranging letters makes different words:

"Add a letter to **phase** to spell **phrase**."

When children are not just adding or changing one letter, cue them to start over.

"Start over and use 5 new letters to spell **phase**."

Give meaning or sentence clues when needed to clarify the word they are making:

"Add 1 letter to spell another word that sounds exactly like **rap** but is spelled differently. I need some paper to **wrap** these presents."

Give children one minute to figure out the secret place and then give clues if needed.

"Our secret place is the name of a state with two words, and we made the first word."

Sort Ph Words

Sort Related Words

Sort Rhymes

Reading Transfer: "Pretend you are reading and come to a new word." Have children put the words under the appropriate rhymes and use the rhymes to decode them.

Spelling Transfer: "Pretend you are writing and need to spell these words." Have children tell you how the words begin. Then, have children find and use the appropriate rhymes to finish spelling the new words.

Step-by-step directions for a sample *Making Places* lesson are on pages 9–13.

New Jersey

e e e j n r s w y __

Make Words: Tell children how many letters to use to make each word. (A slash in the Make Words list indicates that words can be made with the same letters. An underline __ in the letter bank or on the letter strip indicates that a blank space is needed for the secret place.)

Emphasize how changing just one letter or rearranging letters makes different words:

> "Add a letter to **new** to spell **news**."

> "Change 1 letter in **wee** to spell **see**."

> "Use the same letters in **newer** to spell **renew**."

When children are not just adding or changing one letter, cue them to start over.

> "Start over and use 5 new letters to spell **newsy**."

Give meaning or sentence clues when needed to clarify the word they are making:

> "Add 1 letter to spell another word that sounds exactly like **we** but is spelled differently. **Wee** is another word for little. I only weighed five pounds when I was born—I was a **wee**, tiny baby."

Always alert children when they are making a name and expect them to use a capital letter.

> "Take 4 letters and spell **Jews**. Many immigrants to America have been **Jews**."

Give children one minute to figure out the secret place and then give clues if needed.

> "Our secret place is the name of a state with two words, and we made the first word."

Sort Homophones

Sort Related Words

Sort Rhymes

Reading Transfer: "Pretend you are reading and come to a new word." Have children put the words under the appropriate rhymes and use the rhymes to decode them.

Spelling Transfer: "Pretend you are writing and need to spell these words." Have children tell you how the words begin. Then, have children find and use the appropriate rhymes to finish spelling the new words.

Step-by-step directions for a sample *Making Places* lesson are on pages 9–13.

MAKE WORDS

we
wee
see
yes
new
news
Jews
eyes
seen
were
newer/renew
newsy
New Jersey

SORT WORDS

Homophones:
we, wee

Related Words:
new, news, newsy, newer, renew; see, seen

Rhymes:

wee	news
see	Jews

TRANSFER WORDS

Reading:
curfews   disagree

Spelling:
degree   renews

New Mexico

MAKE WORDS

mix
nix
ice
own
mow
mown
come
mice
nice
niece
income
Mexico
New Mexico

SORT WORDS

Related Words:
come, income

Rhymes:
ice   mix   own
nice   nix   mown
mice

TRANSFER WORDS

Reading:
unknown   sacrifice

Spelling:
advice   device

Make Words: Tell children how many letters to use to make each word. (A slash in the Make Words list indicates that words can be made with the same letters. An underline __ in the letter bank or on the letter strip indicates that a blank space is needed for the secret place.)

Emphasize how changing just one letter or rearranging letters makes different words:

"Add a letter to **mow** to spell **mown**."

"Change 1 letter in **mice** to spell **nice**."

When children are not just adding or changing one letter, cue them to start over.

"Start over and use 6 new letters to spell the country of **Mexico**."

Give meaning or sentence clues when needed to clarify the word they are making:

"Start over and use 6 letters to spell **income**. Most people have to pay **income** taxes."

Give children one minute to figure out the secret place and then give clues if needed.

"Our secret place is a state with two words in its name, and we made one of the words."

Sort Related Words

Sort Rhymes

Reading Transfer: "Pretend you are reading and come to a new word." Have children put the words under the appropriate rhymes and use the rhymes to decode them.

Spelling Transfer: "Pretend you are writing and need to spell these words." Have children tell you how the words begin. Then, have children find and use the appropriate rhymes to finish spelling the new words.

Step-by-step directions for a sample *Making Places* lesson are on pages 9–13.

New Orleans

a e e o l n n r s w __

Make Words: Tell children how many letters to use to make each word. (A slash in the Make Words list indicates that words can be made with the same letters. An underline __ in the letter bank or on the letter strip indicates that a blank space is needed for the secret place.)

Emphasize how changing just one letter or rearranging letters makes different words:

> "Add a letter to **ear** to spell **near**."

> "Change 1 letter in **snow** to spell **slow**."

> "Use the same letters in **newer** to spell **renew**."

When children are not just adding or changing one letter, cue them to start over.

> "Start over and use 5 new letters to spell **owner**."

Give meaning or sentence clues when needed to clarify the word they are making:

> "Add 2 letters to spell **renewal**. For their 50th anniversary, my grandparents celebrated with the **renewal** of their wedding vows."

Always alert children when they are making a name and expect them to use a capital letter.

> "Take 5 letters and spell the country of **Wales**. **Wales** is a country in Great Britain."

Give children one minute to figure out the secret place and then give clues if needed.

> "Our secret place is a city in Louisiana where they have Mardi Gras."

Sort Related Words

Sort Rhymes

Reading Transfer: "Pretend you are reading and come to a new word." Have children put the words under the appropriate rhymes and use the rhymes to decode them.

Spelling Transfer: "Pretend you are writing and need to spell these words." Have children tell you how the words begin. Then, have children find and use the appropriate rhymes to finish spelling the new words.

Step-by-step directions for a sample *Making Places* lesson are on pages 9–13.

MAKE WORDS

own
ear
near
Reno
Laos
snow
slow
lose
loser
Wales
owner
newer/renew
renewal
New Orleans

SORT WORDS

Related Words:
newer, renew, renewal;
lose, loser; own, owner
Rhymes:
ear   snow
near   slow

TRANSFER WORDS

Reading:
appear   unknown
Spelling:
disappear   unclear

New York City

e i o c k n r t w y y _ _

▶ MAKE WORDS

no
own
new
not
knot
knew
know
Rick
rock
rocky
Ricky
trick
tricky
New York
New York City

▶ SORT WORDS

Kn Words:
knew, know, knot

Homophones:
knew, new; not, knot; no, know

Related Words:
knew, know; rock, rocky;
trick, tricky

Rhymes:
Rick   Ricky
trick   tricky

▶ TRANSFER WORDS

Reading:
toothpick   sticky

Spelling:
chopstick   picky

Make Words: Tell children how many letters to use to make each word. (A slash in the Make Words list indicates that words can be made with the same letters. An underline __ in the letter bank or on the letter strip indicates that a blank space is needed for the secret place.)

Emphasize how changing just one letter or rearranging letters makes different words:

"Add a letter to **rock** to spell **rocky**."

"Change 1 letter in **knew** to spell **know**."

When children are not just adding or changing one letter, cue them to start over.

"Start over and use 5 new letters to spell **trick**."

Give meaning or sentence clues when needed to clarify the word they are making:

"Add a letter to spell another word that sounds exactly like **not** but is spelled differently. My shoelace has a **knot** in it."

Always alert children when they are making a name and expect them to use a capital letter.

"Take 7 letters and a space and spell the state of **New York**."

Give children one minute to figure out the secret place and then give clues if needed.

"Our secret place is the name of a big city in the state you just spelled."

Sort Kn Words

Sort Homophones

Sort Related Words

Sort Rhymes

Reading Transfer: "Pretend you are reading and come to a new word." Have children put the words under the appropriate rhymes and use the rhymes to decode them.

Spelling Transfer: "Pretend you are writing and need to spell these words." Have children tell you how the words begin. Then, have children find and use the appropriate rhymes to finish spelling the new words.

Step-by-step directions for a sample *Making Places* lesson are on pages 9–13.

New Zealand

a a e e d l n n w z __

Make Words: Tell children how many letters to use to make each word. (A slash in the Make Words list indicates that words can be made with the same letters. An underline __ in the letter bank or on the letter strip indicates that a blank space is needed for the secret place.)

Emphasize how changing just one letter or rearranging letters makes different words:

"Add a letter to **law** to spell **lawn**."

"Change 1 letter in **lend** to spell **lead**."

"Use the same letters in **lead** to spell **deal**."

When children are not just adding or changing one letter, cue them to start over.

"Start over and use 3 new letters to spell **new**."

Give meaning or sentence clues when needed to clarify the word they are making:

"Change 1 letter to spell **zeal**. Our school cheered on the team with a lot of **zeal** and enthusiasm."

Give children one minute to figure out the secret place and then give clues if needed.

"Our secret place is the name of a country with two words, and we made the first word."

Sort Rhymes

Reading Transfer: "Pretend you are reading and come to a new word." Have children put the words under the appropriate rhymes and use the rhymes to decode them.

Spelling Transfer: "Pretend you are writing and need to spell these words." Have children tell you how the words begin. Then, have children find and use the appropriate rhymes to finish spelling the new words.

Step-by-step directions for a sample *Making Places* lesson are on pages 9–13.

Step-by-step directions for a sample *Making Places* lesson are on pages 9–13.

MAKE WORDS

and
new
law
lawn
dawn
land
lend
lead/deal
zeal
New Zealand

SORT WORDS

Rhymes:
and   zeal   lawn
land   deal   dawn

TRANSFER WORDS

Reading:
conceal   reveal

Spelling:
expand   appeal

Nigeria

MAKE WORDS

age
ear
near
gear
Iran/rain
gain
rage
range/anger
regain
Nigeria

SORT WORDS

Related Words:
gain, regain

Rhymes:

age	gain	ear
rage	rain	near
		gear

TRANSFER WORDS

Reading:
terrain   rampage

Spelling:
restrain   engage

Make Words: Tell children how many letters to use to make each word. (A slash in the Make Words list indicates that words can be made with the same letters. An underline __ in the letter bank or on the letter strip indicates that a blank space is needed for the secret place.)

Emphasize how changing just one letter or rearranging letters makes different words:

"Add a letter to **rage** to spell **range**."

"Change 1 letter in **near** to spell **gear**."

"Use the same letters in **range** to spell **anger**."

When children are not just adding or changing one letter, cue them to start over.

"Start over and use 4 letters to spell **rage**."

Give meaning or sentence clues when needed to clarify the word they are making:

"Use 6 letters to spell **regain**. In the sixth inning, the batter hit a home run to **regain** the lead."

Always alert children when they are making a name and expect them to use a capital letter.

"Start over and use 4 new letters to spell the country of **Iran**."

Give children one minute to figure out the secret place and then give clues if needed.

"Our secret place is a country in Africa that begins with **N**."

Sort Related Words

Sort Rhymes

Reading Transfer: "Pretend you are reading and come to a new word." Have children put the words under the appropriate rhymes and use the rhymes to decode them.

Spelling Transfer: "Pretend you are writing and need to spell these words." Have children tell you how the words begin. Then, have children find and use the appropriate rhymes to finish spelling the new words.

Step-by-step directions for a sample *Making Places* lesson are on pages 9–13.

North America

Make Words: Tell children how many letters to use to make each word. (A slash in the Make Words list indicates that words can be made with the same letters. An underline ___ in the letter bank or on the letter strip indicates that a blank space is needed for the secret place.)

Emphasize how changing just one letter or rearranging letters makes different words:

> "Add a letter to **other** to spell **mother**."

When children are not just adding or changing one letter, cue them to start over.

> "Start over and use 6 new letters to spell **camera**."

Give meaning or sentence clues when needed to clarify the word they are making:

> "Start over and use 8 letters to spell **marathon**. He trained for a year so that he could run in the **marathon**."

Always alert children when they are making a name and expect them to use a capital letter.

> "Take 5 letters and spell the country of **China**."

Give children one minute to figure out the secret place and then give clues if needed.

> "Our secret place is a continent with two words in its name, and we made one of the words."

Sort Related Words

Sort Rhymes

Reading Transfer: "Pretend you are reading and come to a new word." Have children put the words under the appropriate rhymes and use the rhymes to decode them.

Spelling Transfer: "Pretend you are writing and need to spell these words." Have children tell you how the words begin. Then, have children find and use the appropriate rhymes to finish spelling the new words.

Step-by-step directions for a sample *Making Places* lesson are on pages 9–13.

MAKE WORDS

arm
harm
hero
charm
China
other
mother
camera
heroic
romance
America
American
marathon
romantic
North America

SORT WORDS

Related Words:
romance, romantic;
America, American;
hero, heroic

Rhymes:
arm   other
harm   mother
charm

TRANSFER WORDS

Reading:
another   alarm

Spelling:
smother   disarm

North Carolina

a a i o o c h l n n r r t __

MAKE WORDS

act
rain
chain
north
nation
notion
lotion
action
cartoon
Ontario
Croatia
Croatian
national
location
North Carolina

SORT WORDS

Words Ending in tion:
nation, notion, action, location, lotion

Related Words:
nation, national; act, action

Rhymes:
notion   rain
lotion   chain

TRANSFER WORDS

Reading:
motion   maintain

Spelling:
potion   restrain

Make Words: Tell children how many letters to use to make each word. (A slash in the Make Words list indicates that words can be made with the same letters. An underline __ in the letter bank or on the letter strip indicates that a blank space is needed for the secret place.)

Emphasize how changing just one letter or rearranging letters makes different words:

> "Add a letter to **Croatia** to spell **Croatian**."

> "Change 1 letter in **notion** to spell **lotion**."

When children are not just adding or changing one letter, cue them to start over.

> "Start over and use 7 new letters to spell **cartoon**."

Give meaning or sentence clues when needed to clarify the word they are making:

> "Start over and use 7 letters to spell **Croatia**. We traveled all over Europe and went to visit our grandparents in **Croatia**."

Always alert children when they are making a name and expect them to use a capital letter.

> "Take 7 letters and spell the city of **Ontario**."

Give children one minute to figure out the secret place and then give clues if needed.

> "Our secret place is a state with two words in its name, and we made one of the words."

Sort Words Ending in tion

Sort Related Words

Sort Rhymes

Reading Transfer: "Pretend you are reading and come to a new word." Have children put the words under the appropriate rhymes and use the rhymes to decode them.

Spelling Transfer: "Pretend you are writing and need to spell these words." Have children tell you how the words begin. Then, have children find and use the appropriate rhymes to finish spelling the new words.

Step-by-step directions for a sample *Making Places* lesson are on pages 9–13.

North Dakota

a a o o d h k n r t t ___

Make Words: Tell children how many letters to use to make each word. (A slash in the Make Words list indicates that words can be made with the same letters. An underline ___ in the letter bank or on the letter strip indicates that a blank space is needed for the secret place.)

Emphasize how changing just one letter or rearranging letters makes different words:

> "Add a letter to **torn** to spell **thorn**."

> "Change 1 letter in **root** to spell **hoot**."

> "Use the same letters in **thorn** to spell **north**."

When children are not just adding or changing one letter, cue them to start over.

> "Start over and use 5 new letters to spell **honor**."

Give meaning or sentence clues when needed to clarify the word they are making:

> "Add 1 letter to spell a different **knot**. I had to get the **knot** out of my shoelace before I could put my sneakers on."

Give children one minute to figure out the secret place and then give clues if needed.

> "Our secret place is a state with two words in its name, and we made one of the words."

Sort Homophones

Sort Rhymes

Reading Transfer: "Pretend you are reading and come to a new word." Have children put the words under the appropriate rhymes and use the rhymes to decode them.

Spelling Transfer: "Pretend you are writing and need to spell these words." Have children tell you how the words begin. Then, have children find and use the appropriate rhymes to finish spelling the new words.

Step-by-step directions for a sample *Making Places* lesson are on pages 9–13.

MAKE WORDS

not
knot
root
hoot
toot
took
nook
torn
thorn/north
honor
aorta
throat
North Dakota

SORT WORDS

Homophones:
not, knot

Rhymes:
root	torn	took
hoot	thorn	nook
toot		

TRANSFER WORDS

Reading:
notebook   newborn

Spelling:
unhook   popcorn

North Korea

a e o o h k n r r t __

MAKE WORDS

take
rake
rank
tank
horn
torn
thorn/north
thank
other
taken
Korea
Korean
another
North Korea

SORT WORDS

Related Words:
Korea, Korean; take, taken;
other, another

Rhymes:

take	horn	tank
rake	torn	thank
	thorn	rank

TRANSFER WORDS

Reading:
popcorn   mistake

Spelling:
acorn   pancake

Make Words: Tell children how many letters to use to make each word. (A slash in the Make Words list indicates that words can be made with the same letters. An underline __ in the letter bank or on the letter strip indicates that a blank space is needed for the secret place.)

Emphasize how changing just one letter or rearranging letters makes different words:

"Add a letter to **torn** to spell **thorn**."

"Change 1 letter in **horn** to spell **torn**."

"Use the same letters in **thorn** to spell **north**."

When children are not just adding or changing one letter, cue them to start over.

"Start over and use 7 new letters to spell **another**."

Give meaning or sentence clues when needed to clarify the word they are making:

"Add 1 letter to **Korea** to spell **Korean**. My grandfather fought in the **Korean** War."

Always alert children when they are making a name and expect them to use a capital letter.

"Take 5 letters and spell **Korea**. After the war, the country of **Korea** was divided into two countries."

Give children one minute to figure out the secret place and then give clues if needed.

"Our secret place is the name of a country with two words, and we made both words."

Sort Related Words

Sort Rhymes

Reading Transfer: "Pretend you are reading and come to a new word." Have children put the words under the appropriate rhymes and use the rhymes to decode them.

Spelling Transfer: "Pretend you are writing and need to spell these words." Have children tell you how the words begin. Then, have children find and use the appropriate rhymes to finish spelling the new words.

Step-by-step directions for a sample *Making Places* lesson are on pages 9–13.

Making Places • CD-104108 • © Carson-Dellosa

North Pole

e o o h l n p r t __

Make Words: Tell children how many letters to use to make each word. (A slash in the Make Words list indicates that words can be made with the same letters. An underline __ in the letter bank or on the letter strip indicates that a blank space is needed for the secret place.)

Emphasize how changing just one letter or rearranging letters makes different words:

> "Change 1 letter in **hoot** to spell **loot**."

> "Use the same letters in **pool** to spell **loop**."

When children are not just adding or changing one letter, cue them to start over.

> "Start over and use 5 letters to spell **hotel**."

Give meaning or sentence clues when needed to clarify the word they are making:

> "Start over and use 7 new letters to spell **pothole**. The car bounced when it ran over the huge **pothole**."

Give children one minute to figure out the secret place and then give clues if needed.

> "Our secret place has two words in its name, and we made both words."

Sort Rhymes

Reading Transfer: "Pretend you are reading and come to a new word." Have children put the words under the appropriate rhymes and use the rhymes to decode them.

Spelling Transfer: "Pretend you are writing and need to spell these words." Have children tell you how the words begin. Then, have children find and use the appropriate rhymes to finish spelling the new words.

Step-by-step directions for a sample *Making Places* lesson are on pages 9–13.

MAKE WORDS

pool/loop
hoop
hoot
loot
pole
hole
hotel
troop
north
photo
phone
throne
pothole
North Pole

SORT WORDS

Rhymes:

pole	hoot	loop	phone
hole	loot	hoop	throne
		troop	

TRANSFER WORDS

Reading:
tombstone   casserole

Spelling:
troubleshoot   postpone

Norway

a o n r w y

MAKE WORDS

an
ran
Roy
Ray
way
now/own/won
war
warn
rayon
Norway

SORT WORDS

Rhymes:
an	Ray
ran	way

TRANSFER WORDS

Reading:
relay   highway

Spelling:
delay   display

Make Words: Tell children how many letters to use to make each word. (A slash in the Make Words list indicates that words can be made with the same letters. An underline __ in the letter bank or on the letter strip indicates that a blank space is needed for the secret place.)

Emphasize how changing just one letter or rearranging letters makes different words:

> "Add a letter to **war** to spell **warn**."

> "Change 1 letter in **Ray** to spell **way**."

> "Use the same letters in **now** to spell **own**. Use these letters again to spell **won**."

When children are not just adding or changing one letter, cue them to start over.

> "Start over and use 3 letters to spell **now**."

Give meaning or sentence clues when needed to clarify the word they are making:

> "Start over and use 5 letters to spell **rayon**. The suit was made from **rayon** and cotton."

Always alert children when they are making a name and expect them to use a capital letter.

> "Take 3 letters and spell the name **Roy**."

Give children one minute to figure out the secret place and then give clues if needed.

> "Our secret place is a country that begins with **N**."

Sort Rhymes

Reading Transfer: "Pretend you are reading and come to a new word." Have children put the words under the appropriate rhymes and use the rhymes to decode them.

Spelling Transfer: "Pretend you are writing and need to spell these words." Have children tell you how the words begin. Then, have children find and use the appropriate rhymes to finish spelling the new words.

Step-by-step directions for a sample *Making Places* lesson are on pages 9–13.

Nova Scotia

a a i o o c n s t v __

Make Words: Tell children how many letters to use to make each word. (A slash in the Make Words list indicates that words can be made with the same letters. An underline __ in the letter bank or on the letter strip indicates that a blank space is needed for the secret place.)

Emphasize how changing just one letter or rearranging letters makes different words:

> "Add a letter to **oats** to spell **coats**."

> "Change 1 letter in **cast** to spell **vast**."

> "Use the same letters in **coats** to spell **coast**. Use the same letters again to spell **tacos**."

When children are not just adding or changing one letter, cue them to start over.

> "Start over and use 6 new letters to spell **action**."

Give meaning or sentence clues when needed to clarify the word they are making:

> "Start over and use 7 letters to spell **ovation**. The concert was wonderful, and everyone gave the band a standing **ovation**."

Give children one minute to figure out the secret place and then give clues if needed.

> "Our secret place is a province in Canada, and the two words begin with **N** and **S**."

Sort Related Words

Sort Rhymes

Reading Transfer: "Pretend you are reading and come to a new word." Have children put the words under the appropriate rhymes and use the rhymes to decode them.

Spelling Transfer: "Pretend you are writing and need to spell these words." Have children tell you how the words begin. Then, have children find and use the appropriate rhymes to finish spelling the new words.

Step-by-step directions for a sample *Making Places* lesson are on pages 9–13.

MAKE WORDS

act
cast
vast
oats
coats/coast/tacos
action
ovation
vacation
vocation
Nova Scotia

SORT WORDS

Related Words:
act, action

Rhymes:
oats   vast
coats   cast

TRANSFER WORDS

Reading:
forecast broadcast

Spelling:
outlast contrast

Oklahoma

a a o o h k l m

MAKE WORDS

am
Al
Hal
ham
oak
look
hook
halo
Alamo
aloha
koala
Oklahoma

SORT WORDS

Rhymes:

am	Al	hook
ham	Hal	look

TRANSFER WORDS

Reading:
canal   scrapbook

Spelling:
fishhook   program

Make Words: Tell children how many letters to use to make each word. (A slash in the Make Words list indicates that words can be made with the same letters. An underline __ in the letter bank or on the letter strip indicates that a blank space is needed for the secret place.)

Emphasize how changing just one letter or rearranging letters makes different words:

> "Add a letter to **Al** to spell the name **Hal**."

> "Change 1 letter in **look** to spell **hook**."

When children are not just adding or changing one letter, cue them to start over.

> "Start over and use 4 letters to spell **halo**."

Give meaning or sentence clues when needed to clarify the word they are making:

> "Start over and use 5 letters to spell **aloha**. In Hawaii, people great each other by saying '**aloha**.'"

Always alert children when they are making a name and expect them to use a capital letter.

> "Take 5 letters and spell a famous place in Texas called the **Alamo**."

Give children one minute to figure out the secret place and then give clues if needed.

> "Our secret place is the name of a state that starts with **O**."

Sort Rhymes

Reading Transfer: "Pretend you are reading and come to a new word." Have children put the words under the appropriate rhymes and use the rhymes to decode them.

Spelling Transfer: "Pretend you are writing and need to spell these words." Have children tell you how the words begin. Then, have children find and use the appropriate rhymes to finish spelling the new words.

Step-by-step directions for a sample *Making Places* lesson are on pages 9–13.

Ontario

a i o o n r t

Make Words: Tell children how many letters to use to make each word. (A slash in the Make Words list indicates that words can be made with the same letters. An underline __ in the letter bank or on the letter strip indicates that a blank space is needed for the secret place.)

Emphasize how changing just one letter or rearranging letters makes different words:

> "Add a letter to **an** to spell **ran**."

> "Change 1 letter in **tin** to spell **ton**."

> "Use the same letters in **riot** to spell **trio**."

When children are not just adding or changing one letter, cue them to start over.

> "Start over and use 5 new letters to spell **ratio**."

Give meaning or sentence clues when needed to clarify the word they are making:

> "Add 1 letter to spell **ration**. During an energy crisis, the government may have to **ration** gasoline."

Give children one minute to figure out the secret place and then give clues if needed.

> "Our secret place is a province in Canada that begins with **O**."

Sort Rhymes

Reading Transfer: "Pretend you are reading and come to a new word." Have children put the words under the appropriate rhymes and use the rhymes to decode them.

Spelling Transfer: "Pretend you are writing and need to spell these words." Have children tell you how the words begin. Then, have children find and use the appropriate rhymes to finish spelling the new words.

Step-by-step directions for a sample *Making Places* lesson are on pages 9–13.

MAKE WORDS

an
ran
tan
tin
ton
Iran
iron
riot/trio
rain
train
ratio
ration
Ontario

SORT WORDS

Rhymes:
an	rain
ran	train
tan	

TRANSFER WORDS

Reading:
obtain   terrain

Spelling:
contain   complain

Orlando

a o o d l n r

MAKE WORDS

an
ran
Dan
Don/nod
rod
and
land
loan
load
road
door/odor
Orlando

SORT WORDS

Rhymes:

an	nod	and	road
Dan	rod	land	load
ran			

TRANSFER WORDS

Reading:
railroad   Superman®

Spelling:
unload   snowman

Make Words: Tell children how many letters to use to make each word. (A slash in the Make Words list indicates that words can be made with the same letters. An underline __ in the letter bank or on the letter strip indicates that a blank space is needed for the secret place.)

Emphasize how changing just one letter or rearranging letters makes different words:

> "Add a letter to **and** to spell **land**."

> "Change 1 letter in **loan** to spell **load**."

> "Use the same letters in **door** to spell **odor**."

When children are not just adding or changing one letter, cue them to start over.

> "Start over and use 3 new letters to spell **and**."

Give meaning or sentence clues when needed to clarify the word they are making:

> "Use the same letters to spell **odor**. What's that terrible **odor** I smell?"

Always alert children when they are making a name and expect them to use a capital letter.

> "Change 1 letter and spell the name **Don**."

Give children one minute to figure out the secret place and then give clues if needed.

> "Our secret place is a city in Florida where Disney World® is."

Sort Rhymes

Reading Transfer: "Pretend you are reading and come to a new word." Have children put the words under the appropriate rhymes and use the rhymes to decode them.

Spelling Transfer: "Pretend you are writing and need to spell these words." Have children tell you how the words begin. Then, have children find and use the appropriate rhymes to finish spelling the new words.

Step-by-step directions for a sample *Making Places* lesson are on pages 9–13.

122

Ottawa, Canada

a a a a a o c d n t t w , __

Make Words: Tell children how many letters to use to make each word. (A slash in the Make Words list indicates that words can be made with the same letters. An underline __ in the letter bank or on the letter strip indicates that a blank space is needed for the secret place.)

Emphasize how changing just one letter or rearranging letters makes different words:

> "Add a letter to **oat** to spell **coat**."

> "Change 1 letter in **down** to spell **dawn**."

> "Use the same letters in **coat** to spell **taco**."

When children are not just adding or changing one letter, cue them to start over.

> "Start over and use 4 letters to spell **want**."

Give meaning or sentence clues when needed to clarify the word they are making:

> "Change 1 letter to spell **wand**. The magician waved his magic **wand**."

Always alert children when they are making a name and expect them to use a capital letter.

> "Take 6 letters and spell the country of **Canada**."

Give children one minute to figure out the secret place and then give clues if needed.

> "Our secret place is a country and its capital, and we spelled the country."

Sort Rhymes

Reading Transfer: "Pretend you are reading and come to a new word." Have children put the words under the appropriate rhymes and use the rhymes to decode them.

Spelling Transfer: "Pretend you are writing and need to spell these words." Have children tell you how the words begin. Then, have children find and use the appropriate rhymes to finish spelling the new words.

Step-by-step directions for a sample *Making Places* lesson are on pages 9–13.

MAKE WORDS

oat
coat/taco
town
down
dawn
data
want
wand
Canada
Ottawa, Canada

SORT WORDS

Rhymes:
oat	down
coat	town

TRANSFER WORDS

Reading:
lifeboat   nightgown

Spelling:
afloat   touchdown

Pacific Ocean

a a e i i o c c c f n p __

MAKE WORDS

ape
ace
ice
nice
face
pace/cape
ocean/canoe
pecan
panic
picnic
icecap
Pacific Ocean

SORT WORDS

Related Words:
ice, icecap

Rhymes:

ice	face	ape
nice	pace	cape
	ace	

TRANSFER WORDS

Reading:
shape   escape

Spelling:
disgrace   landscape

Make Words: Tell children how many letters to use to make each word. (A slash in the Make Words list indicates that words can be made with the same letters. An underline __ in the letter bank or on the letter strip indicates that a blank space is needed for the secret place.)

Emphasize how changing just one letter or rearranging letters makes different words:

"Add a letter to **ice** to spell **nice**."

"Change 1 letter in **face** to spell **pace**."

"Use the same letters in **pace** to spell **cape**."

When children are not just adding or changing one letter, cue them to start over.

"Start over and use 5 new letters to spell **pecan**."

Give meaning or sentence clues when needed to clarify the word they are making:

"Start over and use 6 letters to spell **icecap**. Submarines have gone under the **icecap** at the North Pole."

Give children one minute to figure out the secret place and then give clues if needed.

"Our secret place is an ocean with two words in its name."

Sort Related Words

Sort Rhymes

Reading Transfer: "Pretend you are reading and come to a new word." Have children put the words under the appropriate rhymes and use the rhymes to decode them.

Spelling Transfer: "Pretend you are writing and need to spell these words." Have children tell you how the words begin. Then, have children find and use the appropriate rhymes to finish spelling the new words.

Step-by-step directions for a sample *Making Places* lesson are on pages 9–13.

Pakistan

a a i k n p s t

Make Words: Tell children how many letters to use to make each word. (A slash in the Make Words list indicates that words can be made with the same letters. An underline __ in the letter bank or on the letter strip indicates that a blank space is needed for the secret place.)

Emphasize how changing just one letter or rearranging letters makes different words:

"Add a letter to **tank** to spell **stank**."

"Change 1 letter in **task** to spell **tank**."

"Use the same letters in **sink** to spell **skin**."

When children are not just adding or changing one letter, cue them to start over.

"Start over and use 4 new letters to spell **task**."

Give meaning or sentence clues when needed to clarify the word they are making:

"Change 1 letter to spell **skit**. We performed a **skit** about the explorers."

Always alert children when they are making a name and expect them to use a capital letter.

"Take 4 letters and spell the continent of **Asia**."

Give children one minute to figure out the secret place and then give clues if needed.

"Our secret place is the name of a country that starts with **P**."

Sort Related Words

Sort Rhymes

Reading Transfer: "Pretend you are reading and come to a new word." Have children put the words under the appropriate rhymes and use the rhymes to decode them.

Spelling Transfer: "Pretend you are writing and need to spell these words." Have children tell you how the words begin. Then, have children find and use the appropriate rhymes to finish spelling the new words.

Step-by-step directions for a sample *Making Places* lesson are on pages 9–13.

MAKE WORDS

ask
ink
sink/skin
skip
skit
Asia
task
tank
stank
spank
stink
Pakistan

SORT WORDS

Related Words:
stink, stank

Rhymes:
ink   tank   ask
sink   spank   task
stink   stank

TRANSFER WORDS

Reading:
shrink   shrank

Spelling:
outrank   rethink

Paris, France

a a e i c f n p r r s , __

MAKE WORDS

ape
cape
care
scare
ripe
riper
ripen
safari
France
Africa
scarier
Africans
Paris, France

SORT WORDS

Related Words:
Africa, Africans; scare, scarier;
ripe, riper, ripen

Rhymes:
care   ape
scare   cape

TRANSFER WORDS

Reading:
nightmare   welfare

Spelling:
compare   prepare

Make Words: Tell children how many letters to use to make each word. (A slash in the Make Words list indicates that words can be made with the same letters. An underline __ in the letter bank or on the letter strip indicates that a blank space is needed for the secret place.)

Emphasize how changing just one letter or rearranging letters makes different words:

"Add a letter to **care** to spell **scare**."

"Change 1 letter in **riper** to spell **ripen**."

When children are not just adding or changing one letter, cue them to start over.

"Start over and use 7 new letters to spell **scarier**."

Give meaning or sentence clues when needed to clarify the word they are making:

"Start over and use 6 letters to spell **safari**. I would love to go on a **safari** in Africa and see the animals in their natural habitats."

Always alert children when they are making a name and expect them to use a capital letter.

"Take 6 letters and spell the continent of **Africa**."

Give children one minute to figure out the secret place and then give clues if needed.

"Our secret place is a capital and a country, and we spelled the country."

Sort Related Words

Sort Rhymes

Reading Transfer: "Pretend you are reading and come to a new word." Have children put the words under the appropriate rhymes and use the rhymes to decode them.

Spelling Transfer: "Pretend you are writing and need to spell these words." Have children tell you how the words begin. Then, have children find and use the appropriate rhymes to finish spelling the new words.

Step-by-step directions for a sample *Making Places* lesson are on pages 9–13.

Pennsylvania

a a e i l n n n p s v y

Make Words: Tell children how many letters to use to make each word. (A slash in the Make Words list indicates that words can be made with the same letters. An underline __ in the letter bank or on the letter strip indicates that a blank space is needed for the secret place.)

Emphasize how changing just one letter or rearranging letters makes different words:

> "Add a letter to **live** to spell **alive**."

> "Change 1 letter in **line** to spell **lane**."

When children are not just adding or changing one letter, cue them to start over.

> "Start over and use 6 new letters to spell **easily**."

Give meaning or sentence clues when needed to clarify the word they are making:

> "Take off the **e** and add 2 letters to spell **spinal**. He injured his **spinal** cord in a motorcycle accident."

Always alert children when they are making a name and expect them to use a capital letter.

> "Take 6 letters and spell **Vienna**. **Vienna** is the capital of Austria."

Give children one minute to figure out the secret place and then give clues if needed.

> "Our secret place is a state that begins with the letter **P**."

Sort Related Words

Sort Rhymes

Reading Transfer: "Pretend you are reading and come to a new word." Have children put the words under the appropriate rhymes and use the rhymes to decode them.

Spelling Transfer: "Pretend you are writing and need to spell these words." Have children tell you how the words begin. Then, have children find and use the appropriate rhymes to finish spelling the new words.

Step-by-step directions for a sample *Making Places* lesson are on pages 9–13.

MAKE WORDS

pine
line
lane
sane
easy
live
alive
plane
spine
spinal
easily
Vienna
insane
insanely
Pennsylvania

SORT WORDS

Related Words:
spine, spinal; sane, insane, insanely; easy, easily; live, alive

Rhymes:
pine	lane
line	sane
spine	

TRANSFER WORDS

Reading:
headline   humane

Spelling:
insane   combine

Philadelphia

a a e i i d h h l l p p

128

MAKE WORDS

all
hall
hill
dill
pill
paid
pail
pale
head
ahead
appeal
allied
applied
Philadelphia

SORT WORDS

Homophones:
pail, pale

Related Words:
head, ahead

Rhymes:
hill   all
dill   hall
pill

TRANSFER WORDS

Reading:
downhill   meatball

Spelling:
snowfall   refill

Make Words: Tell children how many letters to use to make each word. (A slash in the Make Words list indicates that words can be made with the same letters. An underline __ in the letter bank or on the letter strip indicates that a blank space is needed for the secret place.)

Emphasize how changing just one letter or rearranging letters makes different words:

"Add a letter to **head** to spell **ahead**."

"Change 1 letter in **dill** to spell **pill**."

When children are not just adding or changing one letter, cue them to start over.

"Start over and use 4 new letters to spell **head**."

Give meaning or sentence clues when needed to clarify the word they are making:

"Use 4 letters to spell a different **pale**. His mother thought he was sick because his face was so **pale**."

Give children one minute to figure out the secret place and then give clues if needed.

"Our secret place is a city in Pennsylvania."

Sort Homophones

Sort Related Words

Sort Rhymes

Reading Transfer: "Pretend you are reading and come to a new word." Have children put the words under the appropriate rhymes and use the rhymes to decode them.

Spelling Transfer: "Pretend you are writing and need to spell these words." Have children tell you how the words begin. Then, have children find and use the appropriate rhymes to finish spelling the new words.

Step-by-step directions for a sample *Making Places* lesson are on pages 9–13.

Philippines

Make Words: Tell children how many letters to use to make each word. (A slash in the Make Words list indicates that words can be made with the same letters. An underline __ in the letter bank or on the letter strip indicates that a blank space is needed for the secret place.)

Emphasize how changing just one letter or rearranging letters makes different words:

"Add a letter to **hip** to spell **ship**."

"Change 1 letter in **shine** to spell **spine**."

When children are not just adding or changing one letter, cue them to start over.

"Start over and use 4 letters to spell **pipe**."

Give meaning or sentence clues when needed to clarify the word they are making:

"Start over and use 7 new letters to spell **hippies**. Some of the students dressed like **hippies**."

Always alert children when they are making a name and expect them to use a capital letter.

"Start over and use 5 new letters to spell the name **Pepsi**®. Do you want **Pepsi**® or Coke®?"

Give children one minute to figure out the secret place and then give clues if needed.

"Our secret place is a country that begins with **Ph**."

Sort Rhymes

Reading Transfer: "Pretend you are reading and come to a new word." Have children put the words under the appropriate rhymes and use the rhymes to decode them.

Spelling Transfer:

"Pretend you are writing and need to spell these words." Have children tell you how the words begin. Then, have children find and use the appropriate rhymes to finish spelling the new words.

Step-by-step directions for a sample *Making Places* lesson are on pages 9–13.

MAKE WORDS

lip
nip
hip
ship
Phil
pipe
pine
line
shine
spine
Pepsi®
hippies
Philippines

SORT WORDS

Rhymes:
pine	hip
line	ship
spine	lip
shine	nip

TRANSFER WORDS

Reading:
outline   tulip

Spelling:
sunshine   unzip

Phoenix, Arizona

a a e i i o o h n n p r x z , __

MAKE WORDS

hope
rope
zero
zone
phone
prize
honor
orphan
horizon
opinion
Arizona
Phoenix, Arizona

SORT WORDS

Rhymes:
zone   hope
phone   rope

TRANSFER WORDS

Reading:
headphone   antelope

Spelling:
postpone   envelope

Make Words: Tell children how many letters to use to make each word. (A slash in the Make Words list indicates that words can be made with the same letters. An underline __ in the letter bank or on the letter strip indicates that a blank space is needed for the secret place.)

Emphasize how changing just one letter or rearranging letters makes different words:

"Change 1 letter in **hope** to spell **rope**."

When children are not just adding or changing one letter, cue them to start over.

"Start over and use 5 new letters to spell **phone**."

Always alert children when they are making a name and expect them to use a capital letter.

"Take 7 letters and spell the state of **Arizona**."

Give meaning or sentence clues when needed to clarify the word they are making:

"Start over and use 7 new letters to spell **horizon**. We sat and watched the sun rise over the **horizon**."

Give children one minute to figure out the secret place and then give clues if needed.

"Our secret place is a capital and its state, and we already spelled the state."

Sort Rhymes

Reading Transfer: "Pretend you are reading and come to a new word." Have children put the words under the appropriate rhymes and use the rhymes to decode them.

Spelling Transfer: "Pretend you are writing and need to spell these words." Have children tell you how the words begin. Then, have children find and use the appropriate rhymes to finish spelling the new words.

Step-by-step directions for a sample *Making Places* lesson are on pages 9–13.

Making Places • CD-104108 • © Carson-Dellosa

Pittsburgh

i u b g h p r s t t

Make Words: Tell children how many letters to use to make each word. (A slash in the Make Words list indicates that words can be made with the same letters. An underline __ in the letter bank or on the letter strip indicates that a blank space is needed for the secret place.)

Emphasize how changing just one letter or rearranging letters makes different words:

"Add a letter to **right** to spell **bright**."

"Change 1 letter in **rush** to spell **gush**."

"Use the same letters in **brush** to spell **shrub**."

When children are not just adding or changing one letter, cue them to start over.

"Start over and use 5 new letters to spell **tight**."

Give meaning or sentence clues when needed to clarify the word they are making:

"Change one letter to spell **uptight**. The couple was very nervous and **uptight** about buying their first house."

Give children one minute to figure out the secret place and then give clues if needed.

"Our secret place is a city in Pennsylvania that begins with **P**."

Sort Related Words

Sort Rhymes

Reading Transfer: "Pretend you are reading and come to a new word." Have children put the words under the appropriate rhymes and use the rhymes to decode them.

Spelling Transfer: "Pretend you are writing and need to spell these words." Have children tell you how the words begin. Then, have children find and use the appropriate rhymes to finish spelling the new words.

Step-by-step directions for a sample *Making Places* lesson are on pages 9–13.

MAKE WORDS

tub
hub
rub
rush
gush
hurt
brush/shrub
spurt
tight
right
bright
upright
uptight
Pittsburgh

SORT WORDS

Related Words:
right, upright; tight, uptight

Rhymes:

right	hub	rush	spurt
tight	rub	gush	hurt
bright	tub	brush	
upright			
uptight			

TRANSFER WORDS

Reading:
eyesight   headlight

Spelling:
flashlight   midnight

Poland

a o d l n p

MAKE WORDS

Al
an
on
Don/nod
and/Dan
pan
pal
plan
land
pond
plod
Poland

SORT WORDS

Rhymes:
an	on	plod	Al	and
Dan	Don	nod	pal	land
pan				
plan				

TRANSFER WORDS

Reading:
understand   Disneyland®

Spelling:
expand   demand

Make Words: Tell children how many letters to use to make each word. (A slash in the Make Words list indicates that words can be made with the same letters. An underline __ in the letter bank or on the letter strip indicates that a blank space is needed for the secret place.)

Emphasize how changing just one letter or rearranging letters makes different words:

"Add a letter to **on** to spell the name **Don**."

"Change 1 letter in **pan** to spell **pal**."

"Use the same letters in **Don** to spell **nod**."

When children are not just adding or changing one letter, cue them to start over.

"Start over and use 4 new letters to spell **pond**."

Give meaning or sentence clues when needed to clarify the word they are making:

"Start over and use 4 letters to spell **plod**. Mowing the lawn was a boring job, but he just had to **plod** along until he finished it."

Always alert children when they are making a name and expect them to use a capital letter.

"Use the same letters to spell the name **Dan**."

Give children one minute to figure out the secret place and then give clues if needed.

"Our secret place is a country that begins with the letter **P**."

Sort Rhymes

Reading Transfer: "Pretend you are reading and come to a new word." Have children put the words under the appropriate rhymes and use the rhymes to decode them.

Spelling Transfer: "Pretend you are writing and need to spell these words." Have children tell you how the words begin. Then, have children find and use the appropriate rhymes to finish spelling the new words.

Step-by-step directions for a sample *Making Places* lesson are on pages 9–13.

Making Places • CD-104108 • © Carson-Dellosa

Portland

a o d l n p r t

Make Words: Tell children how many letters to use to make each word. (A slash in the Make Words list indicates that words can be made with the same letters. An underline __ in the letter bank or on the letter strip indicates that a blank space is needed for the secret place.)

Emphasize how changing just one letter or rearranging letters makes different words:

> "Add a letter to **pant** to spell **plant**."

> "Use the same letters in **prod** to spell **drop**."

When children are not just adding or changing one letter, cue them to start over.

> "Start over and use 5 new letters to spell **adopt**."

Give meaning or sentence clues when needed to clarify the word they are making:

> "Start over and use 6 new letters to spell **pardon**. The prisoner's family asked the governor to **pardon** him."

Always alert children when they are making a name and expect them to use a capital letter.

> "Take 6 letters and spell the country of **Poland**."

Give children one minute to figure out the secret place and then give clues if needed.

> "Our secret place is a city in Oregon and also a city in Maine."

Sort Rhymes

Reading Transfer: "Pretend you are reading and come to a new word." Have children put the words under the appropriate rhymes and use the rhymes to decode them.

Spelling Transfer: "Pretend you are writing and need to spell these words." Have children tell you how the words begin. Then, have children find and use the appropriate rhymes to finish spelling the new words.

Step-by-step directions for a sample *Making Places* lesson are on pages 9–13.

MAKE WORDS

ant
top
nod
prod/drop
port
pant
plant
adopt
polar
pardon
patrol
Poland
Portland

SORT WORDS

Rhymes:
ant	top	nod
pant	drop	prod
plant		

TRANSFER WORDS

Reading:
implant   workshop

Spelling:
transplant   raindrop

Portugal

MAKE WORDS

out
art/rat
rap
lap
lag
lug
plug/gulp
pout
part/trap
polar
patrol
Portugal

SORT WORDS

Rhymes:

out	art	rap	lug
pout	part	trap	plug
		lap	

TRANSFER WORDS

Reading:
ladybug   blackout

Spelling:
unplug   dugout

Make Words: Tell children how many letters to use to make each word. (A slash in the Make Words list indicates that words can be made with the same letters. An underline __ in the letter bank or on the letter strip indicates that a blank space is needed for the secret place.)

Emphasize how changing just one letter or rearranging letters makes different words:

> "Change 1 letter in **lag** to spell **lug**."

> "Use the same letters in **plug** to spell **gulp**."

When children are not just adding or changing one letter, cue them to start over.

> "Start over and use 6 new letters to spell **patrol**."

Give meaning or sentence clues when needed to clarify the word they are making:

> "Start over and use 4 new letters to spell **pout**. You can tell by the **pout** on his face that the little boy did not get what he wanted."

Give children one minute to figure out the secret place and then give clues if needed.

> "Our secret place is a country that begins with the letter **P**."

Sort Rhymes

Reading Transfer: "Pretend you are reading and come to a new word." Have children put the words under the appropriate rhymes and use the rhymes to decode them.

Spelling Transfer: "Pretend you are writing and need to spell these words." Have children tell you how the words begin. Then, have children find and use the appropriate rhymes to finish spelling the new words.

Step-by-step directions for a sample *Making Places* lesson are on pages 9–13.

134

Providence

eeiocdnprv

Make Words: Tell children how many letters to use to make each word. (A slash in the Make Words list indicates that words can be made with the same letters. An underline __ in the letter bank or on the letter strip indicates that a blank space is needed for the secret place.)

Emphasize how changing just one letter or rearranging letters makes different words:

> "Add a letter to **dine** to spell **diner**."

> "Change 1 letter in **vine** to spell **dine**."

> "Use the same letters in **diver** to spell **drive**."

When children are not just adding or changing one letter, cue them to start over.

> "Start over and use 7 new letters to spell **divorce**."

Give meaning or sentence clues when needed to clarify the word they are making:

> "Use 8 letters to spell **province**. Ontario is a **province** in Canada."

Always alert children when they are making a name and expect them to use a capital letter.

> "Take 6 letters and spell the city of **Denver**."

Give children one minute to figure out the secret place and then give clues if needed.

> "Our secret place is the name of the capital of Rhode Island."

Sort Related Words

Sort Rhymes

Reading Transfer: "Pretend you are reading and come to a new word." Have children put the words under the appropriate rhymes and use the rhymes to decode them.

Spelling Transfer: "Pretend you are writing and need to spell these words." Have children tell you how the words begin. Then, have children find and use the appropriate rhymes to finish spelling the new words.

Step-by-step directions for a sample *Making Places* lesson are on pages 9–13.

MAKE WORDS

dive
ripe
vine
dine
diner
diver/drive
prove
proven
Denver
divorce
ripened
province
Providence

SORT WORDS

Related Words:
dive, diver; dine, diner;
ripe, ripened; prove, proven

Rhymes:
dive   dine
drive   vine

TRANSFER WORDS

Reading:
arrive   decline

Spelling:
define   survive

provinces

MAKE WORDS

rope
cope
core
score
scope
since
voice
spice
price
prove
proven
prince
version
provinces

SORT WORDS

Related Words:
prove, proven

Rhymes:

since	core	rope	price
prince	score	scope	spice
			cope

TRANSFER WORDS

Reading:
microscope   restore

Spelling:
explore   telescope

Make Words: Tell children how many letters to use to make each word. (A slash in the Make Words list indicates that words can be made with the same letters. An underline __ in the letter bank or on the letter strip indicates that a blank space is needed for the secret place.)

Emphasize how changing just one letter or rearranging letters makes different words:

"Add a letter to **core** to spell **score**."

"Change 2 letters in **spice** to spell **price**."

When children are not just adding or changing one letter, cue them to start over.

"Start over and use 5 letters to spell **voice**."

Give meaning or sentence clues when needed to clarify the word they are making:

"Use 7 letters to spell **version**. Each person who witnessed the crime told a different **version** of what happened."

Give children one minute to figure out the secret place and then give clues if needed.

"Our secret place refers to the regions that make up Canada. It begins with a lowercase **p**."

Sort Related Words

Sort Rhymes

Reading Transfer: "Pretend you are reading and come to a new word." Have children put the words under the appropriate rhymes and use the rhymes to decode them.

Spelling Transfer: "Pretend you are writing and need to spell these words." Have children tell you how the words begin. Then, have children find and use the appropriate rhymes to finish spelling the new words.

Step-by-step directions for a sample *Making Places* lesson are on pages 9–13.

Puerto Rico

MAKE WORDS

Make Words: Tell children how many letters to use to make each word. (A slash in the Make Words list indicates that words can be made with the same letters. An underline __ in the letter bank or on the letter strip indicates that a blank space is needed for the secret place.)

Emphasize how changing just one letter or rearranging letters makes different words:

"Add a letter to **rice** to spell **price**."

"Change 1 letter in **cure** to spell **pure**."

"Use the same letters in **pure** to spell the country of **Peru**."

When children are not just adding or changing one letter, cue them to start over.

"Start over and use 5 new letters to spell **troop**."

Give meaning or sentence clues when needed to clarify the word they are making:

"Start over and use 7 letters to spell **recruit**. The army officers came to our school to **recruit** people to join the army."

Give children one minute to figure out the secret place and then give clues if needed.

"Our secret place is an island with two words in its name."

Sort Related Words

Sort Rhymes

Reading Transfer: "Pretend you are reading and come to a new word." Have children put the words under the appropriate rhymes and use the rhymes to decode them.

Spelling Transfer: "Pretend you are writing and need to spell these words." Have children tell you how the words begin. Then, have children find and use the appropriate rhymes to finish spelling the new words.

Step-by-step directions for a sample *Making Places* lesson are on pages 9–13.

MAKE WORDS

cure
pure/Peru
rice
price
troop
tropic
trooper
recruit
picture
corrupt
Puerto Rico

SORT WORDS

Related Words:
troop, trooper

Rhymes:
cure   rice
pure   price

TRANSFER WORDS

Reading:
secure   advice

Spelling:
unsure   endure

Rhode Island

a e i o d d h l n r s __

MAKE WORDS

old
sad
hid
hide
hold
slid
slide
older
hidden
sadder
sadden
island
soldier
holders
Rhode Island

SORT WORDS

Related Words:
hid, hide, hidden;
sad, sadder, sadden;
old, older

Rhymes:
old   hid   hide
hold slid slide

TRANSFER WORDS

Reading:
Madrid   household

Spelling:
blindfold   forbid

Make Words: Tell children how many letters to use to make each word. (A slash in the Make Words list indicates that words can be made with the same letters. An underline __ in the letter bank or on the letter strip indicates that a blank space is needed for the secret place.)

Emphasize how changing just one letter or rearranging letters makes different words:

"Add a letter to **hid** to spell **hide**."

When children are not just adding or changing one letter, cue them to start over.

"Start over and use 6 new letters to spell **island**."

Give meaning or sentence clues when needed to clarify the word they are making:

"Change 1 letter to spell **sadden**. She knew the news of her illness would **sadden** everyone."

Give children one minute to figure out the secret place and then give clues if needed.

"Our secret place is a state with two words in its name, and we made one of the words."

Sort Related Words

Sort Rhymes

Reading Transfer: "Pretend you are reading and come to a new word." Have children put the words under the appropriate rhymes and use the rhymes to decode them.

Spelling Transfer: "Pretend you are writing and need to spell these words." Have children tell you how the words begin. Then, have children find and use the appropriate rhymes to finish spelling the new words.

Step-by-step directions for a sample *Making Places* lesson are on pages 9–13.

Making Places • CD-104108 • © Carson-Dellosa

Rome, Italy

a e i o l m r t y , __

Make Words: Tell children how many letters to use to make each word. (A slash in the Make Words list indicates that words can be made with the same letters. An underline __ in the letter bank or on the letter strip indicates that a blank space is needed for the secret place.)

Emphasize how changing just one letter or rearranging letters makes different words:

"Add a letter to **Tim** to spell **time**."

"Change 1 letter in **time** to spell **lime**."

"Use the same letters in **trail** to spell **trial**."

When children are not just adding or changing one letter, cue them to start over.

"Start over and use 7 new letters to spell **reality**."

Always alert children when they are making a name and expect them to use a capital letter.

"Take 5 letters and spell the country of **Italy**."

Give meaning or sentence clues when needed to clarify the word they are making:

"Start over and use 6 new letters to spell **timely**. The **timely** arrival of the firefighter prevented the fire from doing much damage."

Give children one minute to figure out the secret place and then give clues if needed.

"Our secret place is a capital and its country, and we already spelled the country."

Sort Related Words

Sort Rhymes

Reading Transfer: "Pretend you are reading and come to a new word." Have children put the words under the appropriate rhymes and use the rhymes to decode them.

Spelling Transfer: "Pretend you are writing and need to spell these words." Have children tell you how the words begin. Then, have children find and use the appropriate rhymes to finish spelling the new words.

Step-by-step directions for a sample *Making Places* lesson are on pages 9–13.

MAKE WORDS

Tim
time
lime
real
mail
trail/trial
timer
Italy
timely
reality
Rome, Italy

SORT WORDS

Related Words:
time, timer, timely;
real, reality

Rhymes:
time   trail
lime   mail

TRANSFER WORDS

Reading:
pantomime   detail

Spelling:
lifetime   derail

Sacramento

MAKE WORDS

came
same
tame/team
cream
scream
Tacoma
camera
monster
senator
Sacramento

SORT WORDS

Rhymes:

team	came
cream	same
scream	tame

TRANSFER WORDS

Reading:
bloodstream   aflame

Spelling:
overcame   daydream

Make Words: Tell children how many letters to use to make each word. (A slash in the Make Words list indicates that words can be made with the same letters. An underline __ in the letter bank or on the letter strip indicates that a blank space is needed for the secret place.)

Emphasize how changing just one letter or rearranging letters makes different words:

"Add a letter to **cream** to spell **scream**."

"Change 1 letter in **came** to spell **same**."

"Use the same letters in **tame** to spell **team**."

When children are not just adding or changing one letter, cue them to start over.

"Start over and use 7 new letters to spell **monster**."

Give meaning or sentence clues when needed to clarify the word they are making:

"Start over and use 6 letters to spell **Tacoma**. **Tacoma** is a city in Washington."

Give children one minute to figure out the secret place and then give clues if needed.

"Our secret place is the capital of California."

Sort Rhymes

Reading Transfer: "Pretend you are reading and come to a new word." Have children put the words under the appropriate rhymes and use the rhymes to decode them.

Spelling Transfer: "Pretend you are writing and need to spell these words." Have children tell you how the words begin. Then, have children find and use the appropriate rhymes to finish spelling the new words.

Step-by-step directions for a sample *Making Places* lesson are on pages 9–13.

Salem, Oregon

a e e o o g l m n r s , __

Make Words: Tell children how many letters to use to make each word. (A slash in the Make Words list indicates that words can be made with the same letters. An underline __ in the letter bank or on the letter strip indicates that a blank space is needed for the secret place.)

Emphasize how changing just one letter or rearranging letters makes different words:

"Add a letter to **age** to spell **rage**."

"Change 2 letters in **eager** to spell **eagle**."

When children are not just adding or changing one letter, cue them to start over.

"Start over and use 5 new letters to spell **eager**."

Give meaning or sentence clues when needed to clarify the word they are making:

"Use the same letters in **general** to spell **enlarge**. I am going to **enlarge** this photo."

Always alert children when they are making a name and expect them to use a capital letter.

"Take 6 letters and spell the state of **Oregon**."

Give children one minute to figure out the secret place and then give clues if needed.

"Our secret place is a capital and a state, and we already made the state."

Sort Related Words

Sort Rhymes

Reading Transfer: "Pretend you are reading and come to a new word." Have children put the words under the appropriate rhymes and use the rhymes to decode them.

Spelling Transfer: "Pretend you are writing and need to spell these words." Have children tell you how the words begin. Then, have children find and use the appropriate rhymes to finish spelling the new words.

Step-by-step directions for a sample *Making Places* lesson are on pages 9–13.

MAKE WORDS

age
rage
game
name
large
eager
eagle
Oregon
rename
general/enlarge
Salem, Oregon

SORT WORDS

Related Words:
name, rename; large, enlarge

Rhymes:
name   age
game   rage

TRANSFER WORDS

Reading:
inflame   rampage

Spelling:
upstage   became

Salt Lake City

a a e i c k l l s t t y __ __

MAKE WORDS

late
like
easy
sick
stick
skate
Italy
sticky
latest
lately
likely
easily
tackle
tickle
Salt Lake City

SORT WORDS

Related Words:
stick, sticky; like, likely;
easy, easily; late, latest, lately

Rhymes:
late   sick
skate   stick

TRANSFER WORDS

Reading:
vibrate   create

Spelling:
donate   deflate

Make Words: Tell children how many letters to use to make each word. (A slash in the Make Words list indicates that words can be made with the same letters. An underline __ in the letter bank or on the letter strip indicates that a blank space is needed for the secret place.)

Emphasize how changing just one letter or rearranging letters makes different words:

"Add a letter to **sick** to spell **stick**."

"Change 2 letters in **latest** to spell **lately**."

When children are not just adding or changing one letter, cue them to start over.

"Start over and use 6 new letters to spell **tackle**."

Give meaning or sentence clues when needed to clarify the word they are making:

"Use 6 letters to spell **easily**. Our team won the race **easily**."

Always alert children when they are making a name and expect them to use a capital letter.

"Take 5 letters and spell the country of **Italy**."

Give children one minute to figure out the secret place and then give clues if needed.

"Our secret place is the capital of Utah."

Sort Related Words

Sort Rhymes

Reading Transfer: "Pretend you are reading and come to a new word." Have children put the words under the appropriate rhymes and use the rhymes to decode them.

Spelling Transfer: "Pretend you are writing and need to spell these words." Have children tell you how the words begin. Then, have children find and use the appropriate rhymes to finish spelling the new words.

Step-by-step directions for a sample *Making Places* lesson are on pages 9–13.

San Diego

Make Words: Tell children how many letters to use to make each word. (A slash in the Make Words list indicates that words can be made with the same letters. An underline __ in the letter bank or on the letter strip indicates that a blank space is needed for the secret place.)

Emphasize how changing just one letter or rearranging letters makes different words:

"Add a letter to **and** to spell **sand**."

"Use the same letters in **send** to spell **ends**."

When children are not just adding or changing one letter, cue them to start over.

"Start over and use 5 new letters to spell **ideas**."

Give meaning or sentence clues when needed to clarify the word they are making:

"Start over and use 8 letters to spell **diagnose**. The doctor ordered several tests to try to **diagnose** the cause of her illness."

Always alert children when they are making a name and expect them to use a capital letter.

"Take 6 letters and spell a city in Vietnam named **Saigon**."

Give children one minute to figure out the secret place and then give clues if needed.

"Our secret place is a city in California with two words in its name."

Sort Rhymes

Reading Transfer: "Pretend you are reading and come to a new word." Have children put the words under the appropriate rhymes and use the rhymes to decode them.

Spelling Transfer: "Pretend you are writing and need to spell these words." Have children tell you how the words begin. Then, have children find and use the appropriate rhymes to finish spelling the new words.

Step-by-step directions for a sample *Making Places* lesson are on pages 9–13.

MAKE WORDS

an
Dan/and
sand
send/ends
dogs
ideas
design
Saigon
diagnose
San Diego

SORT WORDS

Rhymes:
an   and
Dan   sand

TRANSFER WORDS

Reading:
command   demand

Spelling:
grandstand   expand

San Francisco

a a i o c c f n n r s s ___

MAKE WORDS

far
car
air
fair
Asia
Asian
Oscar
oasis
cross
across
Africa
African
Francis
San Francisco

SORT WORDS

Related Words:
Asia, Asian; Africa, African;
cross, across

Rhymes:
air   car
fair   far

TRANSFER WORDS

Reading:
despair guitar

Spelling:
unfair repair

Make Words: Tell children how many letters to use to make each word. (A slash in the Make Words list indicates that words can be made with the same letters. An underline ___ in the letter bank or on the letter strip indicates that a blank space is needed for the secret place.)

Emphasize how changing just one letter or rearranging letters makes different words:

> "Add a letter to **air** to spell **fair**."

> "Change 1 letter in **far** to spell **car**."

When children are not just adding or changing one letter, cue them to start over.

> "Start over and use 5 new letters to spell the name **Oscar**."

Give meaning or sentence clues when needed to clarify the word they are making:

> "Add 1 letter to **Africa** to spell **African**. We had dinner at an **African** restaurant."

Always alert children when they are making a name and expect them to use a capital letter.

> "Take 4 letters and spell **Asia**. China and India are on the continent of **Asia**."

Give children one minute to figure out the secret place and then give clues if needed.

> "Our secret place is the name of a city in California with two words in its name."

Sort Related Words

Sort Rhymes

Reading Transfer: "Pretend you are reading and come to a new word." Have children put the words under the appropriate rhymes and use the rhymes to decode them.

Spelling Transfer: "Pretend you are writing and need to spell these words." Have children tell you how the words begin. Then, have children find and use the appropriate rhymes to finish spelling the new words.

Step-by-step directions for a sample *Making Places* lesson are on pages 9–13.

Saskatchewan

a a a e c h k n s s t w

Make Words: Tell children how many letters to use to make each word. (A slash in the Make Words list indicates that words can be made with the same letters. An underline __ in the letter bank or on the letter strip indicates that a blank space is needed for the secret place.)

Emphasize how changing just one letter or rearranging letters makes different words:

> "Add a letter to **take** to spell **taken**."

> "Change 1 letter in **wake** to spell **take**."

When children are not just adding or changing one letter, cue them to start over.

> "Start over and use 8 new letters to spell **newscast**."

Give meaning or sentence clues when needed to clarify the word they are making:

> "Take 6 letters and spell **awaken**. I tiptoed into the house because I didn't want to **awaken** anyone."

Always alert children when they are making a name and expect them to use a capital letter.

> "Start over and use 6 new letters to spell the state of **Kansas**."

Give children one minute to figure out the secret place and then give clues if needed.

> "Our secret place is a province in Canada that begins with **S**."

Sort Related Words

Sort Rhymes

Reading Transfer: "Pretend you are reading and come to a new word." Have children put the words under the appropriate rhymes and use the rhymes to decode them.

Spelling Transfer: "Pretend you are writing and need to spell these words." Have children tell you how the words begin. Then, have children find and use the appropriate rhymes to finish spelling the new words.

Step-by-step directions for a sample *Making Places* lesson are on pages 9–13.

MAKE WORDS

new
news
chew
wake
take
taken
awake
shake
shaken
Kansas
awaken
newscast
Saskatchewan

SORT WORDS

Related Words:
new, news, newscast;
wake, awake, awaken;
shake, shaken; take, taken

Rhymes:
take   taken   new
shake   shaken   chew
wake   awaken

TRANSFER WORDS

Reading:
curfew   cashew

Spelling:
outgrew   renew

Saudi Arabia

a a a a i i u b d r s __

MAKE WORDS

sad
bad
bid
rid
Brad/drab
Asia
Arabs
birds
raids
braids
absurd
radius
Saudi Arabia

SORT WORDS

Related Words:
Saudi Arabia, Arabs

Rhymes:
raids	sad	bid
braids	bad	rid
		Brad

TRANSFER WORDS

Reading:
mermaids   pyramid

Spelling:
Madrid   forbid

Make Words: Tell children how many letters to use to make each word. (A slash in the Make Words list indicates that words can be made with the same letters. An underline __ in the letter bank or on the letter strip indicates that a blank space is needed for the secret place.)

Emphasize how changing just one letter or rearranging letters makes different words:

"Add a letter to **raids** to spell **braids**."

"Change 1 letter in **bad** to spell **bid**."

"Use the same letters in **Brad** to spell **drab**."

When children are not just adding or changing one letter, cue them to start over.

"Start over and use 5 new letters to spell **birds**."

Give meaning or sentence clues when needed to clarify the word they are making:

"Use 6 letters to spell **absurd**. Most kids think the idea of not having recess is **absurd**!"

Always alert children when they are making a name and expect them to use a capital letter.

"Take 4 letters and spell the name **Brad**."

Give children one minute to figure out the secret place and then give clues if needed.

"Our secret place is the name of a country, and the two words in its name begin with an **S** and an **A**."

Sort Related Words

Sort Rhymes

Reading Transfer: "Pretend you are reading and come to a new word." Have children put the words under the appropriate rhymes and use the rhymes to decode them.

Spelling Transfer: "Pretend you are writing and need to spell these words." Have children tell you how the words begin. Then, have children find and use the appropriate rhymes to finish spelling the new words.

Step-by-step directions for a sample *Making Places* lesson are on pages 9–13.

Making Places • CD-104108 • © Carson-Dellosa

Scotland

Make Words: Tell children how many letters to use to make each word. (A slash in the Make Words list indicates that words can be made with the same letters. An underline __ in the letter bank or on the letter strip indicates that a blank space is needed for the secret place.)

Emphasize how changing just one letter or rearranging letters makes different words:

"Add a letter to **sand** to spell **stand**."

"Change 1 letter in **toad** to spell **load**."

"Use the same letters in **coats** to spell **coast**. Use these letters again to spell **tacos**."

When children are not just adding or changing one letter, cue them to start over.

"Start over and use 5 new letters to spell **scold**."

Give meaning or sentence clues when needed to clarify the word they are making:

"Change 1 letter to spell **load**. Because the truck carried such a heavy **load**, it could barely climb the mountain."

Give children one minute to figure out the secret place and then give clues if needed.

"Our secret place is a country that begins with the letter **S**."

Sort Rhymes

Reading Transfer: "Pretend you are reading and come to a new word." Have children put the words under the appropriate rhymes and use the rhymes to decode them.

Spelling Transfer: "Pretend you are writing and need to spell these words." Have children tell you how the words begin. Then, have children find and use the appropriate rhymes to finish spelling the new words.

Step-by-step directions for a sample *Making Places* lesson are on pages 9–13.

MAKE WORDS

old
sold
told
cold
toad
load
land
sand
stand
scold
coats/coast/tacos
Scotland

SORT WORDS

Rhymes:

old	toad	sand
sold	load	stand
cold		land
scold		
told		

TRANSFER WORDS

Reading:
crossroad   withhold

Spelling:
overload   unfold

Seattle

a e e l s t t

MAKE WORDS

eat/ate
late
seat/east
least/steal
steel
state/taste
tease
latest
Seattle

SORT WORDS

Homophones:
steel, steal

Related Words:
late, latest

Rhymes:
ate   eat   east
late   seat   least
state

TRANSFER WORDS

Reading:
rotate   retreat

Spelling:
defeat   rebate

Make Words: Tell children how many letters to use to make each word. (A slash in the Make Words list indicates that words can be made with the same letters. An underline __ in the letter bank or on the letter strip indicates that a blank space is needed for the secret place.)

Emphasize how changing just one letter or rearranging letters makes different words:

"Add a letter to **east** to spell **least**."

"Use the same letters in **least** to spell **steal**."

When children are not just adding or changing one letter, cue them to start over.

"Start over and use 6 new letters to spell **latest**."

Give meaning or sentence clues when needed to clarify the word they are making:

"Change 1 letter in **steal** to spell another word that sounds exactly like **steal** but is spelled differently. She bought new stainless **steel** pans."

Give children one minute to figure out the secret place and then give clues if needed.

"Our secret place is a city in Washington that begins with **S**."

Sort Homophones

Sort Related Words

Sort Rhymes

Reading Transfer: "Pretend you are reading and come to a new word." Have children put the words under the appropriate rhymes and use the rhymes to decode them.

Spelling Transfer: "Pretend you are writing and need to spell these words." Have children tell you how the words begin. Then, have children find and use the appropriate rhymes to finish spelling the new words.

Step-by-step directions for a sample *Making Places* lesson are on pages 9–13.

Sierra Leone

a e e e i o l n r r s _

Make Words: Tell children how many letters to use to make each word. (A slash in the Make Words list indicates that words can be made with the same letters. An underline __ in the letter bank or on the letter strip indicates that a blank space is needed for the secret place.)

Emphasize how changing just one letter or rearranging letters makes different words:

> "Add a letter to **earner** to spell **learner**."

> "Change 1 letter in **real** to spell **seal**."

> "Use the same letters in **resale** to spell **reseal**."

When children are not just adding or changing one letter, cue them to start over.

> "Start over and use 6 new letters to spell **resale**."

Give meaning or sentence clues when needed to clarify the word they are making:

> "Use the same letters to spell **relearn**. After the accident, the man had to **relearn** how to walk."

Always alert children when they are making a name and expect them to use a capital letter.

> "Start over and use 4 new letters to spell the country of **Iran**."

Give children one minute to figure out the secret place and then give clues if needed.

> "Our secret place is a country in Africa with two words in its name. The first word begins with **S**, and the second word begins with **L**."

Sort Related Words

Sort Rhymes

Reading Transfer: "Pretend you are reading and come to a new word." Have children put the words under the appropriate rhymes and use the rhymes to decode them.

Spelling Transfer: "Pretend you are writing and need to spell these words." Have children tell you how the words begin. Then, have children find and use the appropriate rhymes to finish spelling the new words.

Step-by-step directions for a sample *Making Places* lesson are on pages 9–13.

MAKE WORDS

real
seal/sale
Iran
earn
learn
resale/reseal
earner
learner/relearn
Sierra Leone

SORT WORDS

Related Words:
sale, resale; seal, reseal;
earn, earner;
learn, learner, relearn

Rhymes:
| real | earn | earner |
| seal | learn | learner |

TRANSFER WORDS

Reading:
ordeal   reveal

Spelling:
squeal   ideal

Singapore

a e i o g n p r s

MAKE WORDS

ape
ripe
gripe
grape
ripen
ponies
person
region
Saigon
pigeons
oranges
Singapore

SORT WORDS

Related Words:
ripe, ripen

Rhymes:
ripe   ape
gripe   grape

TRANSFER WORDS

Reading:
landscape   bagpipe

Spelling:
unripe   escape

Make Words: Tell children how many letters to use to make each word. (A slash in the Make Words list indicates that words can be made with the same letters. An underline __ in the letter bank or on the letter strip indicates that a blank space is needed for the secret place.)

Emphasize how changing just one letter or rearranging letters makes different words:

> "Add a letter to **ripe** to spell **gripe**."

> "Change a letter in **gripe** to spell **grape**."

When children are not just adding or changing one letter, cue them to start over.

> "Start over and use 6 new letters to spell **ponies**."

Give meaning or sentence clues when needed to clarify the word they are making:

> "Start over and use 6 new letters to spell **region**. What **region** of the country do you live in?"

Always alert children when they are making a name and expect them to use a capital letter.

> "Take 6 letters and spell the city of **Saigon**."

Give children one minute to figure out the secret place and then give clues if needed.

> "Our secret place is a country in Asia that begins with **S**."

Sort Related Words

Sort Rhymes

Reading Transfer: "Pretend you are reading and come to a new word." Have children put the words under the appropriate rhymes and use the rhymes to decode them.

Spelling Transfer: "Pretend you are writing and need to spell these words." Have children tell you how the words begin. Then, have children find and use the appropriate rhymes to finish spelling the new words.

Step-by-step directions for a sample *Making Places* lesson are on pages 9–13.

Making Places • CD-104108 • © Carson-Dellosa

South Africa

a a i o u c f h r s t __

Make Words: Tell children how many letters to use to make each word. (A slash in the Make Words list indicates that words can be made with the same letters. An underline __ in the letter bank or on the letter strip indicates that a blank space is needed for the secret place.)

Emphasize how changing just one letter or rearranging letters makes different words:

> "Add a letter to **cart** to spell **chart**."

When children are not just adding or changing one letter, cue them to start over.

> "Start over and use 7 new letters to spell **haircut**."

Give meaning or sentence clues when needed to clarify the word they are making:

> "Start over and use 6 new letters to spell **fourth**. She came in **fourth** place out of a hundred in the race."

Always alert children when they are making a name and expect them to use a capital letter.

> "Take 4 letters and spell the continent of **Asia**."

Give children one minute to figure out the secret place and then give clues if needed.

> "Our secret place is a country with two words in its name. We made both words."

Sort Related Words

Sort Rhymes

Reading Transfer: "Pretend you are reading and come to a new word." Have children put the words under the appropriate rhymes and use the rhymes to decode them.

Spelling Transfer: "Pretend you are writing and need to spell these words." Have children tell you how the words begin. Then, have children find and use the appropriate rhymes to finish spelling the new words.

Step-by-step directions for a sample *Making Places* lesson are on pages 9–13.

MAKE WORDS

four
Asia
hair
cart
chart
chair
south
Africa
fourth
haircut
Croatia
South Africa

SORT WORDS

Related Words:
hair, haircut; four, fourth

Rhymes:
hair   cart
chair   chart

TRANSFER WORDS

Reading:
despair   outsmart

Spelling:
repair   apart

South America

aaeiouchmrst _

MAKE WORDS

arch
atom
Asia
race
tour
march
teach
reach
racist
racism
tourism
America
outreach
amateurs
South America

SORT WORDS

Related Words:
race, racism, racist;
tour, tourism;
reach, outreach

Rhymes:
arch   teach
march   reach
         outreach

TRANSFER WORDS

Reading:
starch   impeach

Spelling:
bleach   parch

Make Words: Tell children how many letters to use to make each word. (A slash in the Make Words list indicates that words can be made with the same letters. An underline __ in the letter bank or on the letter strip indicates that a blank space is needed for the secret place.)

Emphasize how changing just one letter or rearranging letters makes different words:

"Change a letter in **teach** to spell **reach**."

When children are not just adding or changing one letter, cue them to start over.

"Start over and use 6 new letters to spell **racist**."

Give meaning or sentence clues when needed to clarify the word they are making:

"Start over and use 8 letters to spell **outreach**. Most of the churches in town have **outreach** programs for the community."

Always alert children when they are making a name and expect them to use a capital letter.

"Take 4 letters and spell the continent of **Asia**."

Give children one minute to figure out the secret place and then give clues if needed.

"Our secret place is a continent with two words in its name."

Sort Related Words

Sort Rhymes

Reading Transfer: "Pretend you are reading and come to a new word." Have children put the words under the appropriate rhymes and use the rhymes to decode them.

Spelling Transfer: "Pretend you are writing and need to spell these words." Have children tell you how the words begin. Then, have children find and use the appropriate rhymes to finish spelling the new words.

Step-by-step directions for a sample *Making Places* lesson are on pages 9–13.

South Carolina

a a i o o u c h l n r s t ___

Make Words: Tell children how many letters to use to make each word. (A slash in the Make Words list indicates that words can be made with the same letters. An underline ___ in the letter bank or on the letter strip indicates that a blank space is needed for the secret place.)

Emphasize how changing just one letter or rearranging letters makes different words:

> "Add a letter to **action** to spell **auction**."

> "Change 1 letter in **rash** to spell **rush**."

> "Use the same letters in **auction** to spell **caution**."

When children are not just adding or changing one letter, cue them to start over.

> "Start over and use 8 new letters to spell **solution**."

Give meaning or sentence clues when needed to clarify the word they are making:

> "Start over and use 9 letters to spell **atrocious**. His handwriting was not just bad; it was **atrocious**."

Always alert children when they are making a name and expect them to use a capital letter.

> "Take 4 letters and spell the country of **Laos**."

Give children one minute to figure out the secret place and then give clues if needed.

> "Our secret place is a state with two words in its name, and we made one of the words."

Sort Related Words

Sort Rhymes

Reading Transfer: "Pretend you are reading and come to a new word." Have children put the words under the appropriate rhymes and use the rhymes to decode them.

Spelling Transfer: "Pretend you are writing and need to spell these words." Have children tell you how the words begin. Then, have children find and use the appropriate rhymes to finish spelling the new words.

Step-by-step directions for a sample *Making Places* lesson are on pages 9–13.

MAKE WORDS

hair
Ohio
Laos
rash
rush
crush
crash
south
action
auction/caution
haircut
solution
atrocious
South Carolina

SORT WORDS

Related Words:
hair, haircut

Rhymes:
rush   rash
crush   crash

TRANSFER WORDS

Reading:
hairbrush   whiplash
Spelling:
eyelash   toothbrush

South Dakota

a a o o u d h k s t t __

▶ MAKE WORDS

do
dot
hot
hoot
hook
hood
soda
auto
Otto
outdo
shook
shoot
stood
south
South Dakota

▶ SORT WORDS

Related Words:
do, outdo

Rhymes:
dot	hoot	hook	hood
hot	shoot	shook	stood

▶ TRANSFER WORDS

Reading:
mascot   checkbook

Spelling:
outlook   jackpot

Make Words: Tell children how many letters to use to make each word. (A slash in the Make Words list indicates that words can be made with the same letters. An underline __ in the letter bank or on the letter strip indicates that a blank space is needed for the secret place.)

Emphasize how changing just one letter or rearranging letters makes different words:

"Add a letter to **hot** to spell **hoot**."

"Change 1 letter in **hoot** to spell **hook**."

When children are not just adding or changing one letter, cue them to start over.

"Start over and use 5 new letters to spell **shook**."

Give meaning or sentence clues when needed to clarify the word they are making:

"Start over and use 5 letters to spell **outdo**. He was always trying to **outdo** his older sister."

Always alert children when they are making a name and expect them to use a capital letter.

"Take 4 letters and spell the name **Otto**."

Give children one minute to figure out the secret place and then give clues if needed.

"Our secret place is a state with two words in its name, and we made one of the words."

Sort Related Words

Sort Rhymes

Reading Transfer: "Pretend you are reading and come to a new word." Have children put the words under the appropriate rhymes and use the rhymes to decode them.

Spelling Transfer: "Pretend you are writing and need to spell these words." Have children tell you how the words begin. Then, have children find and use the appropriate rhymes to finish spelling the new words.

Step-by-step directions for a sample *Making Places* lesson are on pages 9–13.

Making Places • CD-104108 • © Carson-Dellosa

South Korea

a e o o u h k r s t __

Make Words: Tell children how many letters to use to make each word. (A slash in the Make Words list indicates that words can be made with the same letters. An underline __ in the letter bank or on the letter strip indicates that a blank space is needed for the secret place.)

Emphasize how changing just one letter or rearranging letters makes different words:

"Add a letter to **skate** to spell **skater**."

"Change 1 letter in **root** to spell **hoot**."

"Use the same letters in **earth** to spell **heart**."

When children are not just adding or changing one letter, cue them to start over.

"Start over and use 7 new letters to spell **shooter**."

Give meaning or sentence clues when needed to clarify the word they are making:

"Use 6 letter to spell **shaker**. Could you please fill the pepper **shaker**?"

Always alert children when they are making a name and expect them to use a capital letter.

"Use the same letters and spell the name **Kate**."

Give children one minute to figure out the secret place and then give clues if needed.

"Our secret place is the name of a country with two words, and we made the first word."

Sort Related Words

Sort Rhymes

Reading Transfer: "Pretend you are reading and come to a new word." Have children put the words under the appropriate rhymes and use the rhymes to decode them.

Spelling Transfer: "Pretend you are writing and need to spell these words." Have children tell you how the words begin. Then, have children find and use the appropriate rhymes to finish spelling the new words.

Step-by-step directions for a sample *Making Places* lesson are on pages 9–13.

MAKE WORDS

take/Kate
root
hoot
shoot
south
earth/heart
shoot
shake
skate
skater
shaker
shooter
South Korea

SORT WORDS

Related Words:
skate, skater; shoot, shooter; shake, shaker

Rhymes:
root   take   Kate
hoot   shake   skate
shoot

TRANSFER WORDS

Reading:
rotate   uproot

Spelling:
cupcake   debate

South Pole

e o o u h l p s t __

MAKE WORDS

out
pout
pole
hole
pool
tool
tools/stool
south/shout
upset/setup
photos
potholes
South Pole

SORT WORDS

Related Words:
hole, potholes

Rhymes:
pool   out   pole
tool   pout   hole
stool   shout

TRANSFER WORDS

Reading:
workout   school

Spelling:
tadpole   cookout

Make Words: Tell children how many letters to use to make each word. (A slash in the Make Words list indicates that words can be made with the same letters. An underline __ in the letter bank or on the letter strip indicates that a blank space is needed for the secret place.)

Emphasize how changing just one letter or rearranging letters makes different words:

> "Add a letter to **tool** to spell **tools**."

> "Change 1 letter in **pool** to spell **tool**."

> "Use the same letters in **upset** to spell **setup**."

When children are not just adding or changing one letter, cue them to start over.

> "Start over and use 6 new letters to spell **photos**."

Give meaning or sentence clues when needed to clarify the word they are making:

> "Start over and use 8 new letters to spell **potholes**. The road crews were out fixing the **potholes** in the streets."

Give children one minute to figure out the secret place and then give clues if needed.

> "Our secret place is a place with two words in its name, and we made both words."

Sort Related Words

Sort Rhymes

Reading Transfer: "Pretend you are reading and come to a new word." Have children put the words under the appropriate rhymes and use the rhymes to decode them.

Spelling Transfer: "Pretend you are writing and need to spell these words." Have children tell you how the words begin. Then, have children find and use the appropriate rhymes to finish spelling the new words.

Step-by-step directions for a sample *Making Places* lesson are on pages 9–13.

156

Making Places • CD-104108 • © Carson-Dellosa

states

Make Words: Tell children how many letters to use to make each word. (A slash in the Make Words list indicates that words can be made with the same letters. An underline __ in the letter bank or on the letter strip indicates that a blank space is needed for the secret place.)

Emphasize how changing just one letter or rearranging letters makes different words:

> "Add a letter to **eat** to spell **east**."

> "Change 1 letter in **sat** to spell **set**."

> "Use the same letters in **east** to spell **seat**."

When children are not just adding or changing one letter, cue them to start over.

> "Start over and use 5 new letters to spell **taste**."

Give meaning or sentence clues when needed to clarify the word they are making:

> "Change 1 letter to spell **sea**. Fish and people swim in the **sea**."

Give children one minute to figure out the secret words and give clues if needed.

> "Today we have two secret words, and both start with lowercase letters. The first word is not a place, but the other one is. You can make one secret word by adding a letter to **taste**. The other secret word is the kind of place that California, North Carolina, and Rhode Island are."

Sort Rhymes

Reading Transfer: "Pretend you are reading and come to a new word." Have children put the words under the appropriate rhymes and use the rhymes to decode them.

Spelling Transfer: "Pretend you are writing and need to spell these words." Have children tell you how the words begin. Then, have children find and use the appropriate rhymes to finish spelling the new words.

Step-by-step directions for a sample *Making Places* lesson are on pages 9–13.

MAKE WORDS

at
sat
set
sea
tea/ate/eat
east/seat
taste
tastes/states

SORT WORDS

Rhymes:
at	sea	eat
sat	tea	seat

TRANSFER WORDS

Reading:
retreat   acrobat

Spelling:
repeat   democrat

Sweden

MAKE WORDS

end/den/Ned
dew
new
news
seed
weed
need
send
dense
Sweden

SORT WORDS

Related Words:
new, news

Rhymes:
end	seed	dew
send	weed	new
	need	

TRANSFER WORDS

Reading:
succeed   pretend

Spelling:
exceed   extend

Make Words: Tell children how many letters to use to make each word. (A slash in the Make Words list indicates that words can be made with the same letters. An underline __ in the letter bank or on the letter strip indicates that a blank space is needed for the secret place.)

Emphasize how changing just one letter or rearranging letters makes different words:

> "Add a letter to **new** to spell **news**."

> "Change 1 letter in **seed** to spell **weed**."

> "Use the same letters in **end** to spell **den**."

When children are not just adding or changing one letter, cue them to start over.

> "Start over and use 4 new letters to spell **seed**."

Give meaning or sentence clues when needed to clarify the word they are making:

> "Start over and use 5 letters to spell **dense**. It was hard walking through the jungle because the underbrush was so **dense**."

Always alert children when they are making a name and expect them to use a capital letter.

> "Use these same letters again and spell the name **Ned**."

Give children one minute to figure out the secret place and then give clues if needed.

> "Our secret place is country that begins with **S**."

Sort Related Words

Sort Rhymes

Reading Transfer: "Pretend you are reading and come to a new word." Have children put the words under the appropriate rhymes and use the rhymes to decode them.

Spelling Transfer: "Pretend you are writing and need to spell these words." Have children tell you how the words begin. Then, have children find and use the appropriate rhymes to finish spelling the new words.

Step-by-step directions for a sample *Making Places* lesson are on pages 9–13.

Switzerland

a e i d l n r s t w z

Make Words: Tell children how many letters to use to make each word. (A slash in the Make Words list indicates that words can be made with the same letters. An underline __ in the letter bank or on the letter strip indicates that a blank space is needed for the secret place.)

Emphasize how changing just one letter or rearranging letters makes different words:

> "Add a letter to **wide** to spell **wider**."

> "Add a letter to **and** to spell **land**."

When children are not just adding or changing one letter, cue them to start over.

> "Start over and use 4 new letters to spell **wild**."

Give meaning or sentence clues when needed to clarify the word they are making:

> "Use 8 letters to spell **wetlands**. The **wetlands** habitat was home to alligators."

Always alert children when they are making a name and expect them to use a capital letter.

> "Take 7 letters and spell the country of **Ireland**."

Give children one minute to figure out the secret place and then give clues if needed.

> "Our secret place is a country that begins with **S**."

Sort Related Words

Sort Rhymes

Reading Transfer: "Pretend you are reading and come to a new word." Have children put the words under the appropriate rhymes and use the rhymes to decode them.

Spelling Transfer: "Pretend you are writing and need to spell these words." Have children tell you how the words begin. Then, have children find and use the appropriate rhymes to finish spelling the new words.

Step-by-step directions for a sample *Making Places* lesson are on pages 9–13.

MAKE WORDS

and
land
wild
side
wide
wider
Wales
widest
wilder
wildest
Ireland
wetlands
Switzerland

SORT WORDS

Related Words:
wild, wilder, wildest;
wide, wider, widest

Rhymes:
and   side
land   wide

TRANSFER WORDS

Reading:
command   decide

Spelling:
divide   demand

Tallahassee

MAKE WORDS

eat
see
sea
seal
heal
heel
heat
sell
east
least
shell
seashell
Tallahassee

SORT WORDS

Homophones:
see, sea; heel, heal

Related Words:
see, sea; heel, heal;
shell, seashell

Rhymes:

eat	seal	east	sell
heat	heal	least	shell
			seashell

TRANSFER WORDS

Reading:
bombshell   ideal

Spelling:
oatmeal   misspell

Make Words: Tell children how many letters to use to make each word. (A slash in the Make Words list indicates that words can be made with the same letters. An underline __ in the letter bank or on the letter strip indicates that a blank space is needed for the secret place.)

Emphasize how changing just one letter or rearranging letters makes different words:

"Add a letter to **sea** to spell **seal**."

"Change 1 letter in **see** to spell the **sea** that means ocean."

When children are not just adding or changing one letter, cue them to start over.

"Start over and use 5 new letters to spell **shell**."

Give meaning or sentence clues when needed to clarify the word they are making:

"Change one letter to spell another word that sounds exactly like **heal** but is spelled differently. I fell and cut my **heel**."

Give children one minute to figure out the secret place and then give clues if needed.

"Our secret place is the capital of Florida and begins with a **T**."

Sort Homophones

Sort Related Words

Sort Rhymes

Reading Transfer: "Pretend you are reading and come to a new word." Have children put the words under the appropriate rhymes and use the rhymes to decode them.

Spelling Transfer: "Pretend you are writing and need to spell these words." Have children tell you how the words begin. Then, have children find and use the appropriate rhymes to finish spelling the new words.

Step-by-step directions for a sample *Making Places* lesson are on pages 9–13.

Tennessee

Make Words: Tell children how many letters to use to make each word. (A slash in the Make Words list indicates that words can be made with the same letters. An underline __ in the letter bank or on the letter strip indicates that a blank space is needed for the secret place.)

Emphasize how changing just one letter or rearranging letters makes different words:

"Change 1 letter in **teen** to spell **seen**."

"Use the same letters in **tense** to spell **teens**."

When children are not just adding or changing one letter, cue them to start over.

"Start over and use 4 new letters to spell **teen**."

Give meaning or sentence clues when needed to clarify the word they are making:

"Change 1 letter in **sense** to spell **tense**. The students and teachers were all **tense** as the time for the state tests approached."

Give children one minute to figure out the secret place and then give clues if needed.

"Our secret place is the name of a state that starts with **T**."

Sort Related Words

Sort Rhymes

Reading Transfer: "Pretend you are reading and come to a new word." Have children put the words under the appropriate rhymes and use the rhymes to decode them.

Spelling Transfer: "Pretend you are writing and need to spell these words." Have children tell you how the words begin. Then, have children find and use the appropriate rhymes to finish spelling the new words.

Step-by-step directions for a sample *Making Places* lesson are on pages 9–13.

MAKE WORDS

see
ten/net
set
sent/nets/nest
teen
seen
sense
tense/teens
Tennessee

SORT WORDS

Related Words:
see, seen; teen, teens;
net, nets

Rhymes:

net	teen	sense
set	seen	tense

TRANSFER WORDS

Reading:
offense   intense

Spelling:
suspense   defense

Thailand

a a i d h l n t

MAKE WORDS

hid
lid
lad
had
Dan/and
hand
land
than
thin
nail
tail
hail
Diana
Thailand

SORT WORDS

Rhymes:

hid	and	lad	nail	Dan
lid	hand	had	tail	than
	land		hail	

TRANSFER WORDS

Reading:
expand   detail

Spelling:
hybrid   prevail

Make Words: Tell children how many letters to use to make each word. (A slash in the Make Words list indicates that words can be made with the same letters. An underline __ in the letter bank or on the letter strip indicates that a blank space is needed for the secret place.)

Emphasize how changing just one letter or rearranging letters makes different words:

"Add a letter to **and** to spell **hand**."

"Change 1 letter in **than** to spell **thin**."

"Use the same letters in **Dan** to spell **and**."

When children are not just adding or changing one letter, cue them to start over.

"Start over and use 4 new letters to spell **than**."

Give meaning or sentence clues when needed to clarify the word they are making:

"Change 1 letter to spell **hail**. The storm had dangerous lightning and **hail** the size of golf balls."

Always alert children when they are making a name and expect them to use a capital letter.

"Take 5 letters and spell the name **Diana**."

Give children one minute to figure out the secret place and then give clues if needed.

"Our secret place is a country that begins with **T**."

Sort Rhymes

Reading Transfer: "Pretend you are reading and come to a new word." Have children put the words under the appropriate rhymes and use the rhymes to decode them.

Spelling Transfer: "Pretend you are writing and need to spell these words." Have children tell you how the words begin. Then, have children find and use the appropriate rhymes to finish spelling the new words.

Step-by-step directions for a sample *Making Places* lesson are on pages 9–13.

Tokyo, Japan

Make Words: Tell children how many letters to use to make each word. (A slash in the Make Words list indicates that words can be made with the same letters. An underline __ in the letter bank or on the letter strip indicates that a blank space is needed for the secret place.)

Emphasize how changing just one letter or rearranging letters makes different words:

> "Change 1 letter in **tank** to spell **yank**."

> "Use the same letters in **Tokyo** to spell the city of **Kyoto**."

When children are not just adding or changing one letter, cue them to start over.

> "Start over and use 4 new letters to spell **pony**."

Give meaning or sentence clues when needed to clarify the word they are making:

> "Add 1 letter to spell another word that sounds exactly like **not** but is spelled differently. Can you help me get the **knot** out of my shoe?"

Always alert children when they are making a name and expect them to use a capital letter.

> "Change 1 letter to spell the name **Kay**."

Give children one minute to figure out the secret place and then give clues if needed.

> "Our secret place is the name of a capital and a country, and we already made the capital."

Sort Homophones

Sort Rhymes

Reading Transfer: "Pretend you are reading and come to a new word." Have children put the words under the appropriate rhymes and use the rhymes to decode them.

Spelling Transfer: "Pretend you are writing and need to spell these words." Have children tell you how the words begin. Then, have children find and use the appropriate rhymes to finish spelling the new words.

Step-by-step directions for a sample *Making Places* lesson are on pages 9–13.

MAKE WORDS

pay
Kay
Jay
joy
toy
not
knot
tank
yank
pony
Tokyo/Kyoto
Tokyo, Japan

SORT WORDS

Homophones:
not, knot

Rhymes:
pay	joy	tank
Kay	toy	yank
Jay		

TRANSFER WORDS

Reading:
annoy   delay

Spelling:
subway   enjoy

Topeka, Kansas

a a a e o k k n p s s t , __

MAKE WORDS

take/Kate
skate/steak/stake
snake
spoke
spoken
Kansas
peasants
Topeka, Kansas

SORT WORDS

Related Words:
spoke, spoken

Rhymes:
take   Kate
stake   skate
snake

TRANSFER WORDS

Reading:
tailgate   stagnate
Spelling:
dominate   candidate

Make Words: Tell children how many letters to use to make each word. (A slash in the Make Words list indicates that words can be made with the same letters. An underline __ in the letter bank or on the letter strip indicates that a blank space is needed for the secret place.)

Emphasize how changing just one letter or rearranging letters makes different words:

"Add a letter to **spoke** to spell **spoken**."

"Use the same letters in **skate** to spell **steak.** Do you like to eat **steak**?"

"Use these letters again to spell another word that sounds exactly like **steak** but is spelled differently. Each scout member put a **stake** in the ground to hold up the tent."

When children are not just adding or changing one letter, cue them to start over.

"Start over and use 5 letters to spell **spoke**."

Always alert children when they are making a name and expect them to use a capital letter.

"Take 6 letters and spell the state of **Kansas**."

Give meaning or sentence clues when needed to clarify the word they are making:

"Start over and use 8 new letters to spell **peasants**. The **peasants** worked hard farming the land and caring for the animals."

Give children one minute to figure out the secret place and then give clues if needed.

"Our secret place is a capital and its state, and we already spelled the state."

Sort Related Words

Sort Rhymes

Reading Transfer: "Pretend you are reading and come to a new word." Have children put the words under the appropriate rhymes and use the rhymes to decode them.

Spelling Transfer: "Pretend you are writing and need to spell these words." Have children tell you how the words begin. Then, have children find and use the appropriate rhymes to finish spelling the new words.

Step-by-step directions for a sample *Making Places* lesson are on pages 9–13.

164

United States

a e e i u d n s s t t t __

Make Words: Tell children how many letters to use to make each word. (A slash in the Make Words list indicates that words can be made with the same letters. An underline __ in the letter bank or on the letter strip indicates that a blank space is needed for the secret place.)

Emphasize how changing just one letter or rearranging letters makes different words:

> "Change 1 letter in **test** to spell **nest**."

> "Use the same letters in **untie** to spell **unite**."

When children are not just adding or changing one letter, cue them to start over.

> "Start over and use 6 new letters to spell **senate**."

Give meaning or sentence clues when needed to clarify the word they are making:

> "Change 1 letter in **untested** to spell **untasted**. No one had much of an appetite after the candidate lost, so lots of wonderful food went **untasted**."

Give children one minute to figure out the secret place and then give clues if needed.

> "Our secret place is the name of a country in North America."

Sort Related Words

Sort Rhymes

Reading Transfer: "Pretend you are reading and come to a new word." Have children put the words under the appropriate rhymes and use the rhymes to decode them.

Spelling Transfer: "Pretend you are writing and need to spell these words." Have children tell you how the words begin. Then, have children find and use the appropriate rhymes to finish spelling the new words.

Step-by-step directions for a sample *Making Places* lesson are on pages 9–13.

MAKE WORDS

tie
test
nest
date
state/taste
untie/unite
senate
dentist
students
untested
untasted
attitudes
United States

SORT WORDS

Related Words:
tie, untie; test, untested;
taste, untasted

Rhymes:
test   date
nest   state

TRANSFER WORDS

Reading:
protest   decorate

Spelling:
request   integrate

Vancouver

a e o u c n r v v

MAKE WORDS

cane
cave
rave
crave/carve
curve
crane
ocean
cover
uncover
Vancouver

SORT WORDS

Related Words:
cover, uncover

Rhymes:
cave   cane
rave   crane
crave

TRANSFER WORDS

Reading:
microwave   engrave

Spelling:
behave   forgave

Make Words: Tell children how many letters to use to make each word. (A slash in the Make Words list indicates that words can be made with the same letters. An underline __ in the letter bank or on the letter strip indicates that a blank space is needed for the secret place.)

Emphasize how changing just one letter or rearranging letters makes different words:

"Add a letter to **rave** to spell **crave**."

"Change 1 letter in **carve** to spell **curve**."

"Use the same letters in **crave** to spell **carve**."

When children are not just adding or changing one letter, cue them to start over.

"Start over and use 5 new letters to spell **ocean**."

Give meaning or sentence clues when needed to clarify the word they are making:

"Add 2 letters to **cover** to spell **uncover**. The detective wanted to **uncover** the clues that would solve the case."

Give children one minute to figure out the secret place and then give clues if needed.

"Our secret place is a city in Canada that begins with **V**."

Sort Related Words

Sort Rhymes

Reading Transfer: "Pretend you are reading and come to a new word." Have children put the words under the appropriate rhymes and use the rhymes to decode them.

Spelling Transfer: "Pretend you are writing and need to spell these words." Have children tell you how the words begin. Then, have children find and use the appropriate rhymes to finish spelling the new words.

Step-by-step directions for a sample *Making Places* lesson are on pages 9–13.

Vatican City

a a i i c c n t t v y __

Make Words: Tell children how many letters to use to make each word. (A slash in the Make Words list indicates that words can be made with the same letters. An underline __ in the letter bank or on the letter strip indicates that a blank space is needed for the secret place.)

Emphasize how changing just one letter or rearranging letters makes different words:

"Add a letter to **can** to spell the name **Cain**."

"Change 1 letter in **van** to spell **can**."

When children are not just adding or changing one letter, cue them to start over.

"Start over and use 5 new letters to spell **attic**."

Give meaning or sentence clues when needed to clarify the word they are making:

"Use 7 letters to spell **vacancy**. On big football weekends, all of the hotels had 'No **Vacancy**' signs."

Always alert children when they are making a name and expect them to use a capital letter.

"Take 7 letters and spell the ship named **Titanic**."

Give children one minute to figure out the secret place and then give clues if needed.

"Our secret place is the name of a tiny country, and we made the last word in its name."

Sort Related Words

Sort Rhymes

Reading Transfer: "Pretend you are reading and come to a new word." Have children put the words under the appropriate rhymes and use the rhymes to decode them.

Spelling Transfer: "Pretend you are writing and need to spell these words." Have children tell you how the words begin. Then, have children find and use the appropriate rhymes to finish spelling the new words.

Step-by-step directions for a sample *Making Places* lesson are on pages 9–13.

MAKE WORDS

act
van
can
Cain
vain
city
navy
attic
vanity
cavity
vacant
vacancy
Titanic
activity
Vatican City

SORT WORDS

Related Words:
vacant, vacancy; act, activity; vain, vanity

Rhymes:
van   Cain
can   vain

TRANSFER WORDS

Reading:
entertain   restrain

Spelling:
explain   complain

Venezuela

a e e e u l n v z

MAKE WORDS

van
vane
lane/lean
veal
zeal
value
avenue
eleven
Venezuela

SORT WORDS

Rhymes:
vane   veal
lane   zeal

TRANSFER WORDS

Reading:
airplane   oatmeal

Spelling:
insane   conceal

Make Words: Tell children how many letters to use to make each word. (A slash in the Make Words list indicates that words can be made with the same letters. An underline __ in the letter bank or on the letter strip indicates that a blank space is needed for the secret place.)

Emphasize how changing just one letter or rearranging letters makes different words:

"Add a letter to **van** to spell **vane**."

"Change 1 letter in **veal** to spell **zeal**."

"Use the same letters in **lane** to spell **lean**."

When children are not just adding or changing one letter, cue them to start over.

"Start over and use 5 new letters to spell **value**."

Give meaning or sentence clues when needed to clarify the word they are making:

"Use 6 letters to spell **avenue**. The parade was on Fifth **Avenue**."

Give children one minute to figure out the secret place and then give clues if needed.

"Our secret place is a country in South America that begins with **V**."

Sort Rhymes

Reading Transfer: "Pretend you are reading and come to a new word." Have children put the words under the appropriate rhymes and use the rhymes to decode them.

Spelling Transfer: "Pretend you are writing and need to spell these words." Have children tell you how the words begin. Then, have children find and use the appropriate rhymes to finish spelling the new words.

Step-by-step directions for a sample *Making Places* lesson are on pages 9–13.

Venice, Italy

a e e i i c l n t v y , __

Make Words: Tell children how many letters to use to make each word. (A slash in the Make Words list indicates that words can be made with the same letters. An underline __ in the letter bank or on the letter strip indicates that a blank space is needed for the secret place.)

Emphasize how changing just one letter or rearranging letters makes different words:

> "Add a letter to **live** to spell **alive**."

> "Change 1 letter in **lice** to spell **lace**."

When children are not just adding or changing one letter, cue them to start over.

> "Start over and use 6 new letters to spell **nicely**."

Give meaning or sentence clues when needed to clarify the word they are making:

> "Add 2 letters to spell **inactive**. I couldn't get on the Internet because my account was **inactive**."

Always alert children when they are making a name and expect them to use a capital letter.

> "Take 5 letters and spell the country of **Italy**."

Give children one minute to figure out the secret place and then give clues if needed.

> "Our secret place is the name of a city and a country, and we already made the country."

Sort Related Words

Sort Rhymes

Reading Transfer: "Pretend you are reading and come to a new word." Have children put the words under the appropriate rhymes and use the rhymes to decode them.

Spelling Transfer: "Pretend you are writing and need to spell these words." Have children tell you how the words begin. Then, have children find and use the appropriate rhymes to finish spelling the new words.

Step-by-step directions for a sample *Making Places* lesson are on pages 9–13.

MAKE WORDS

act
ace
ice
nice
lice
lace
live
alive
Italy
nicely
invite
active
inactive
actively
Venice, Italy

SORT WORDS

Related Words:
act, active, inactive, actively;
nice, nicely; live, alive

Rhymes:
ace	ice
lace	nice
	lice

TRANSFER WORDS

Reading:
sacrifice   misplace

Spelling:
replace   advice

Vermont

e o m n r t v

MAKE WORDS

rent
vent
veto/vote
note
mote
more
tore
torn
Rome
move
mover
voter
venom
Vermont

SORT WORDS

Related Words:
vote, voter; move, mover;
tore, torn

Rhymes:

vote	more	rent
note	tore	vent
mote		

TRANSFER WORDS

Reading:
therefore   promote

Spelling:
seashore   devote

Make Words: Tell children how many letters to use to make each word. (A slash in the Make Words list indicates that words can be made with the same letters. An underline __ in the letter bank or on the letter strip indicates that a blank space is needed for the secret place.)

Emphasize how changing just one letter or rearranging letters makes different words:

"Add a letter to **move** to spell **mover**."

"Change 1 letter in **mote** to spell **more**."

"Use the same letters in **veto** to spell **vote**."

When children are not just adding or changing one letter, cue them to start over.

"Start over and use 5 new letters to spell **voter**."

Give meaning or sentence clues when needed to clarify the word they are making:

"Use 5 letters to spell **venom**. The **venom** from the snakebite almost killed him."

Always alert children when they are making a name and expect them to use a capital letter.

"Start over and use 4 new letters to spell the city of **Rome**. **Rome** is the capital of Italy."

Give children one minute to figure out the secret place and then give clues if needed.

"Our secret place is a state whose name begins with **V**."

Sort Related Words

Sort Rhymes

Reading Transfer: "Pretend you are reading and come to a new word." Have children put the words under the appropriate rhymes and use the rhymes to decode them.

Spelling Transfer: "Pretend you are writing and need to spell these words." Have children tell you how the words begin. Then, have children find and use the appropriate rhymes to finish spelling the new words.

Step-by-step directions for a sample *Making Places* lesson are on pages 9–13.

Vietnam

a e i m n t v

Make Words: Tell children how many letters to use to make each word. (A slash in the Make Words list indicates that words can be made with the same letters. An underline __ in the letter bank or on the letter strip indicates that a blank space is needed for the secret place.)

Emphasize how changing just one letter or rearranging letters makes different words:

> "Add a letter to **man** to spell **mean**."

> "Change 1 letter in **name** to spell **tame**."

> "Use the same letters in **mean** to spell **name**."

When children are not just adding or changing one letter, cue them to start over.

> "Start over and use 6 new letters to spell **native**."

Give meaning or sentence clues when needed to clarify the word they are making:

> "Use 4 letters to spell a different **vane**. In science class, we made a weather **vane**. Use 4 letters again to spell another **vain**. When someone thinks he is the very best, we say he is **vain**."

Give children one minute to figure out the secret place and then give clues if needed.

> "Our secret place is a country in Asia that begins with **V**."

Sort Homophones

Sort Related Words

Sort Rhymes

Reading Transfer: "Pretend you are reading and come to a new word." Have children put the words under the appropriate rhymes and use the rhymes to decode them.

Spelling Transfer: "Pretend you are writing and need to spell these words." Have children tell you how the words begin. Then, have children find and use the appropriate rhymes to finish spelling the new words.

Step-by-step directions for a sample *Making Places* lesson are on pages 9–13.

MAKE WORDS

van
man
mean/name
tame
time
mine
vine/vein
vane
vain
meant
native
Vietnam

SORT WORDS

Homophones:
vein, vane, vain

Related Words:
mean, meant

Rhymes:
van   name
man   tame

TRANSFER WORDS

Reading:
nickname   Japan

Spelling:
became   dishpan

Virginia

a i i i g n r v

MAKE WORDS

in
an
van
ran
rag
nag
air
ring/grin
Iran/rain
gain
grain
airing
Virginia

SORT WORDS

Related Words:
air, airing

Rhymes:

an	in	rag	rain
van	grin	nag	gain
ran			grain
Iran			

TRANSFER WORDS

Reading:
sustain   pertain

Spelling:
explain   complain

Make Words: Tell children how many letters to use to make each word. (A slash in the Make Words list indicates that words can be made with the same letters. An underline __ in the letter bank or on the letter strip indicates that a blank space is needed for the secret place.)

Emphasize how changing just one letter or rearranging letters makes different words:

"Add a letter to **gain** to spell **grain**."

"Change 1 letter in **rain** to spell **gain**."

"Use the same letters in **ring** to spell **grin**."

When children are not just adding or changing one letter, cue them to start over.

"Start over and use 4 new letters to spell **Iran**."

Give meaning or sentence clues when needed to clarify the word they are making:

"Start over and use 6 new letters to spell **airing**. She was **airing** the quilts by hanging them on the clothesline."

Always alert children when they are making a name and expect them to use a capital letter.

"Take 4 letters and spell the country of **Iran**."

Give children one minute to figure out the secret place and then give clues if needed.

"Our secret place is a state that begins with the letter **V**."

Sort Related Words

Sort Rhymes

Reading Transfer: "Pretend you are reading and come to a new word." Have children put the words under the appropriate rhymes and use the rhymes to decode them.

Spelling Transfer: "Pretend you are writing and need to spell these words." Have children tell you how the words begin. Then, have children find and use the appropriate rhymes to finish spelling the new words.

Step-by-step directions for a sample *Making Places* lesson are on pages 9–13.

Washington

a i o g h n n s t w

Make Words: Tell children how many letters to use to make each word. (A slash in the Make Words list indicates that words can be made with the same letters. An underline ___ in the letter bank or on the letter strip indicates that a blank space is needed for the secret place.)

Emphasize how changing just one letter or rearranging letters makes different words:

> "Add a letter to **show** to spell **shown**."

> "Change 1 letter in **snow** to spell **stow**."

When children are not just adding or changing one letter, cue them to start over.

> "Start over and use 6 new letters to spell **sawing**."

Give meaning or sentence clues when needed to clarify the word they are making:

> "Use 4 letters to spell **thaw**. The sun came out, and the ice began to **thaw**."

Give children one minute to figure out the secret place and then give clues if needed.

> "Our secret place is the name of a state and a city and can be made by adding your letters to **washing**."

Sort Related Words

Sort Rhymes

Reading Transfer: "Pretend you are reading and come to a new word." Have children put the words under the appropriate rhymes and use the rhymes to decode them.

Spelling Transfer: "Pretend you are writing and need to spell these words." Have children tell you how the words begin. Then, have children find and use the appropriate rhymes to finish spelling the new words.

Step-by-step directions for a sample *Making Places* lesson are on pages 9–13.

MAKE WORDS

saw
thaw
wash
snow
stow
show
shown
sawing
thawing
snowing
stowing
showing
nations
washing
Washington

SORT WORDS

Related Words:
saw, sawing; thaw, thawing; stow, stowing; snow, snowing; show, shown, showing; wash, washing

Rhymes:

saw	snow	sawing	snowing
thaw	stow	thawing	stowing
	show		showing

TRANSFER WORDS

Reading:
withdraw   growing

Spelling:
blowing   outlaw

West Virginia

MAKE WORDS

rain
wave
rave
stain
anger
write
waving
raving
starve
writing
rainiest
angriest
starving
Virginia
West Virginia

SORT WORDS

Related Words:
wave, waving; rave, raving;
write, writing; starve, starving;
rain, rainiest; anger, angriest

Rhymes:
rain   rave   waving
stain   wave   raving

TRANSFER WORDS

Reading:
maintain   craving
Spelling:
paving   restrain

Make Words: Tell children how many letters to use to make each word. (A slash in the Make Words list indicates that words can be made with the same letters. An underline __ in the letter bank or on the letter strip indicates that a blank space is needed for the secret place.)

Emphasize how changing just one letter or rearranging letters makes different words:

> "Change 1 letter in **waving** to spell **raving**."

When children are not just adding or changing one letter, cue them to start over.

> "Start over and use 7 new letters to spell **writing**."

Give meaning or sentence clues when needed to clarify the word they are making:

> "Start over and use 8 letters to spell **angriest**. Everyone was angry about the oil spill, but the fishermen who fished the water there were the **angriest**."

Always alert children when they are making a name and expect them to use a capital letter.

> "Take 8 letters and spell the state of **Virginia**."

Give children one minute to figure out the secret place and then give clues if needed.

> "Our secret place is the name of a state with two words, and we made one of the words."

Sort Related Words and point out that **e** is dropped when **-ing** is added.

Sort Rhymes

Reading Transfer: "Pretend you are reading and come to a new word." Have children put the words under the appropriate rhymes and use the rhymes to decode them.

Spelling Transfer: "Pretend you are writing and need to spell these words." Have children tell you how the words begin. Then, have children find and use the appropriate rhymes to finish spelling the new words.

Step-by-step directions for a sample *Making Places* lesson are on pages 9–13.

Wisconsin

i i o c n n s s w

Make Words: Tell children how many letters to use to make each word. (A slash in the Make Words list indicates that words can be made with the same letters. An underline ___ in the letter bank or on the letter strip indicates that a blank space is needed for the secret place.)

Emphasize how changing just one letter or rearranging letters makes different words:

> "Add a letter to **in** to spell **win**."

> "Change 1 letter in **win** to spell **won**."

> "Use the same letters in **won** to spell **own**."

When children are not just adding or changing one letter, cue them to start over.

> "Start over and use 5 new letters to spell **snows**."

Give meaning or sentence clues when needed to clarify the word they are making:

> "Change 1 letter to spell **sow**. The **sow** took good care of her little baby pigs."

Give children one minute to figure out the secret place and then give clues if needed.

> "Our secret place is the name of a state that starts with **W**."

Sort Related Words

Sort Rhymes

Reading Transfer: "Pretend you are reading and come to a new word." Have children put the words under the appropriate rhymes and use the rhymes to decode them.

Spelling Transfer: "Pretend you are writing and need to spell these words." Have children tell you how the words begin. Then, have children find and use the appropriate rhymes to finish spelling the new words.

Step-by-step directions for a sample *Making Places* lesson are on pages 9–13.

MAKE WORDS

in
win
won/own/now
sow
cow
owns
snows
coins
Wisconsin

SORT WORDS

Related Words:
win, won; own, owns

Rhymes:

in	now
win	sow
	cow

TRANSFER WORDS

Reading:
allow   Moscow

Spelling:
snowplow   somehow

Wyoming

MAKE WORDS

in
win
wig
gym
won/own
mow
mown
wing
Yogi
owing
mowing
Wyoming

SORT WORDS

Related Words:
mow, mown, mowing

Rhymes:
in   own   owing
win   mown   mowing

TRANSFER WORDS

Reading:
blowing   windblown

Spelling:
overgrown   growing

Make Words: Tell children how many letters to use to make each word. (A slash in the Make Words list indicates that words can be made with the same letters. An underline __ in the letter bank or on the letter strip indicates that a blank space is needed for the secret place.)

Emphasize how changing just one letter or rearranging letters makes different words:

"Add a letter to **owing** to spell **mowing**."

"Change 1 letter in **win** to spell **wig**."

"Use the same letters in **won** to spell **own**."

When children are not just adding or changing one letter, cue them to start over.

"Start over and use 5 new letters to spell **owing**."

Give meaning or sentence clues when needed to clarify the word they are making:

"Add 1 letter to spell **mown**. I love the smell of newly **mown** grass."

Always alert children when they are making a name and expect them to use a capital letter.

"Take 4 letters and spell the name **Yogi**."

Give children one minute to figure out the secret place and then give clues if needed.

"Our secret place is the name of a state that starts with **W**."

Sort Related Words

Sort Rhymes

Reading Transfer: "Pretend you are reading and come to a new word." Have children put the words under the appropriate rhymes and use the rhymes to decode them.

Spelling Transfer: "Pretend you are writing and need to spell these words." Have children tell you how the words begin. Then, have children find and use the appropriate rhymes to finish spelling the new words.

Step-by-step directions for a sample *Making Places* lesson are on pages 9–13.

Places Index

Geographic Place*	Lesson(s) Containing That Place
Afghanistan	Afghanistan
Africa	California—Paris, France—San Francisco—South Africa
African	California—San Francisco
Africans	Paris, France
Alaska	Juneau, Alaska
Albany	Albany, New York
Alberta	Alberta
Albuquerque	Albuquerque
America	North America—South America
American	North America
Ankara	Arkansas
Antarctica	Antarctica
Arabs	Nebraska—Saudi Arabia
Arctic	Antarctica
Arctic Ocean	Arctic Ocean
Argentina	Argentina
Arizona	Phoenix, Arizona
Arkansas	Arkansas
Asia	Afghanistan—Austin, Texas—Australia—Louisiana—Pakistan—San Francisco—Saudi Arabia—South Africa—South America
Asian	San Francisco
Athens	Athens, Greece—Charleston
Atlanta	Atlantic Ocean
Atlantic Ocean	Atlantic Ocean
atlas	Australia
Augusta	Augusta, Maine
Austin	Austin, Texas
Australia	Australia
Austria	Australia
Baltimore	Baltimore
Baton Rouge	Baton Rouge
beach	Beijing, China
Beijing	Beijing, China

* General geographic terms and related place terms are italicized.

Places Index

Geographic Place*	Lesson(s) Containing That Place
Birmingham	Birmingham
Boise	Boise, Idaho
Boston	Boston
British	British Columbia
British Columbia	British Columbia
Cairo	Cairo, Egypt—Moscow, Russia
California	California
Canada	Ottawa, Canada
canal	California
capitals	capitals
Charleston	Charleston
Charlotte	Charlotte
Chile	Lake Michigan
China	Beijing, China—Michigan—North America
city	Jefferson City—Kansas City—Mexico City—Vatican City
Cleveland	Cleveland
coast	Charleston—Scotland
Colombia	Colombia
Colorado	Colorado
Columbus	Columbus, Ohio
Connecticut	Connecticut
continents	continents
counties	countries
countries	countries
Croatia	Arctic Ocean—North Carolina—South Africa
Croatian	North Carolina
Delaware	Delaware
Denmark	Denmark
Denver	Providence
Des Moines	Des Moines, Iowa
Earth	Earth
east	Seattle—states—Tallahassee
Egypt	Cairo, Egypt

* General geographic terms and related place terms are italicized.

Geographic Place*	Lesson(s) Containing That Place
England	England—Greenland—London, England
Europe	Lake Superior
Florida	Florida
France	Paris, France
Georgia	Georgia
German	Germany
Germany	Germany
Great Britain	Great Britain
Greece	Athens, Greece
Greenland	Greenland
Hawaii	Honolulu, Hawaii
Helena	Helena, Montana
Honolulu	Honolulu, Hawaii
Houston	Houston
Hungary	Hungary
icecap	Pacific Ocean
Idaho	Boise, Idaho
Illinois	Illinois
India	Indiana—Indianapolis—Indian Ocean—Indonesia—Madrid, Spain
Indian	Indiana—Indianapolis—Indian Ocean
Indiana	Indiana—Indianapolis—Indian Ocean
Indianapolis	Indianapolis
Indian Ocean	Indian Ocean
Indians	Indonesia
Indonesia	Indonesia
inlet	Atlantic Ocean
Iowa	Des Moines, Iowa—Honolulu, Hawaii—Moscow, Russia
Iran	Antarctica—Birmingham—Ireland—Nigeria—Ontario—Sierra Leone—Virginia
Ireland	Ireland—Switzerland
island	Indianapolis—Rhode Island
islands	islands
Israel	Israel

* General geographic terms and related place terms are italicized.

Geographic Place*	Lesson(s) Containing That Place
Italy	Rome, Italy—Salt Lake City—Venice, Italy
Jackson	Jackson
Japan	Tokyo, Japan
Jefferson City	Jefferson City
Jerusalem	Jerusalem
Juneau	Juneau, Alaska
Kansas	Arkansas—Kansas City—Saskatchewan—Topeka, Kansas
Kansas City	Kansas City
Kentucky	Kentucky
Korea	Albany, New York—Lake Huron—Lake Ontario—North Korea
Korean	Albany, New York—Lake Huron—Lake Ontario—North Korea
Kyoto	Tokyo, Japan
lake	Juneau, Alaska—Lake Erie—Lake Huron—Lake Superior
Lake Erie	Lake Erie
Lake Huron	Lake Huron
Lake Michigan	Lake Michigan
Lake Ontario	Lake Ontario
Lake Superior	Lake Superior
land	England—New Zealand—Orlando—Poland—Scotland—Switzerland—Thailand
Laos	Indianapolis—Los Angeles—Louisiana—New Orleans—South Carolina
Laotian	Atlantic Ocean—Lake Ontario
Las Vegas	Las Vegas
Latino	Atlantic Ocean—Lake Ontario
Lebanon	Albany, New York
Liberia	Liberia
Lima	Colombia
Little Rock	Little Rock
location	North Carolina
London	London, England
Los Angeles	Los Angeles
Louisiana	Louisiana

* General geographic terms and related place terms are italicized.

Geographic Place*	Lesson(s) Containing That Place
Madrid	Madrid, Spain
Maine	Augusta, Maine—Minneapolis—Minnesota—New Hampshire
Manitoba	Manitoba
marina	Madrid, Spain
Maryland	Maryland
Massachusetts	Massachusetts
Mexico	Mexico City—New Mexico
Mexico City	Mexico City
Miami	Birmingham
Michigan	Lake Michigan—Michigan
Minneapolis	Minneapolis
Minnesota	Minnesota
Montana	Helena, Montana—Montana
Montgomery	Montgomery
Montreal	Montreal
Moscow	Moscow, Russia
mountains	mountains
Nashville	Nashville
nation	Atlantic Ocean—Minnesota—mountains—North Carolina
national	Atlantic Ocean—North Carolina
nations	nations—Washington
native	Vietnam
Nebraska	Nebraska
New Brunswick	New Brunswick
New Hampshire	New Hampshire
New Jersey	New Jersey
New Mexico	New Mexico
New Orleans	New Orleans
New York	Albany, New York—New York City
New York City	New York City
New Zealand	New Zealand
Newfoundland	Newfoundland
Nigeria	Great Britain–Nigeria

* General geographic terms and related place terms are italicized.

Geographic Place*	Lesson(s) Containing That Place
north	North Carolina—North Dakota—North Korea—North Pole
North America	North America
North Carolina	North Carolina
North Dakota	North Dakota
North Korea	North Korea
North Pole	North Pole
Norway	Albany, New York—Norway
Nova Scotia	Nova Scotia
oasis	San Francisco
ocean	Arctic Ocean—Atlantic Ocean—Charleston—Pacific Ocean—Vancouver
Ohio	Columbus, Ohio—Honolulu, Hawaii—South Carolina
Oklahoma	Oklahoma
Ontario	Lake Ontario—North Carolina—Ontario
Oregon	Montgomery—Salem, Oregon
Orlando	Orlando
Ottawa	Ottawa, Canada
Pacific Ocean	Pacific Ocean
Pakistan	Pakistan
Paris	Lake Superior—Madrid, Spain—New Hampshire—Paris, France
Parisian	Madrid, Spain
Pennsylvania	Pennsylvania
Peru	Puerto Rico
Philadelphia	Philadelphia
Philippines	Philippines
Phoenix	Phoenix, Arizona
Pittsburgh	Pittsburgh
Poland	Indianapolis—Poland—Portland
polar	Portland—Portugal
port	Portland
Portland	Portland
Portugal	Portugal
Providence	Providence

* General geographic terms and related place terms are italicized.

Geographic Place*	Lesson(s) Containing That Place
province	Providence
provinces	provinces
Puerto Rico	Puerto Rico
region	Singapore
Reno	Baton Rouge—Charleston—countries—New Orleans
Rhode Island	Rhode Island
Rome	Baltimore—Montgomery—Montreal—Rome, Italy—Vermont
Russia	Moscow, Russia
Sacramento	Sacramento
Saigon	San Diego—Singapore
Salem	Jerusalem—Salem, Oregon
Salt Lake City	Salt Lake City
San Diego	San Diego
San Francisco	San Francisco
Saskatchewan	Saskatchewan
Saudi Arabia	Saudi Arabia
Scotland	Scotland
sea	states—Tallahassee
Seattle	Seattle
Sierra Leone	Sierra Leone
Singapore	Singapore
south	Houston—South Africa—South Carolina—South Dakota—South Korea—South Pole
South Africa	South Africa
South America	South America
South Carolina	South Carolina
South Dakota	South Dakota
South Korea	South Korea
South Pole	South Pole
Spain	Indianapolis—Madrid, Spain
state	United States
states	Austin, Texas—states
Sweden	Des Moines, Iowa—Sweden

* General geographic terms and related place terms are italicized.

* General geographic terms and related place terms are italicized.

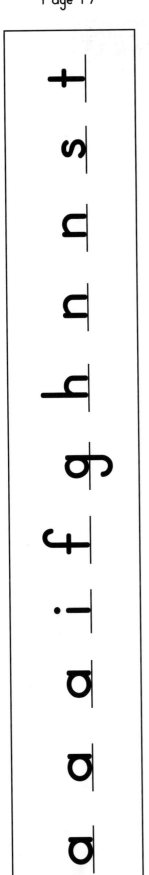

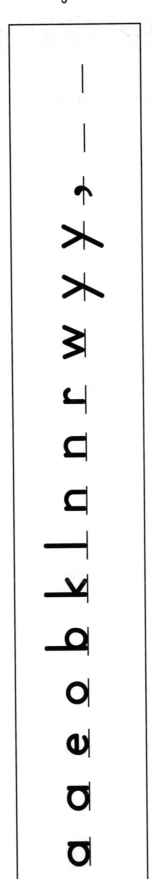

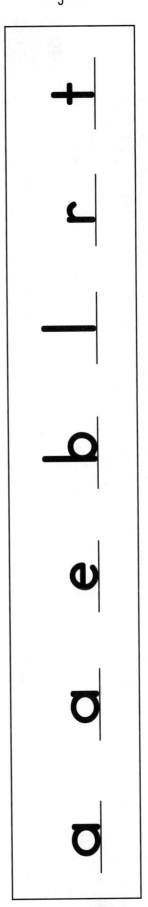

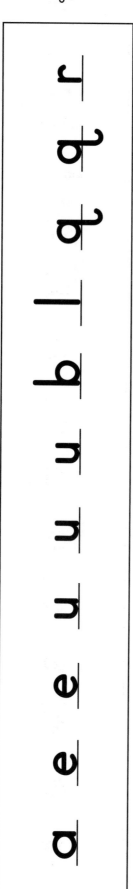

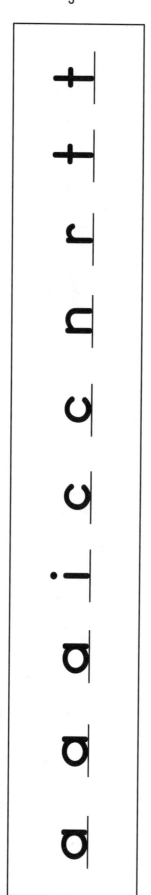

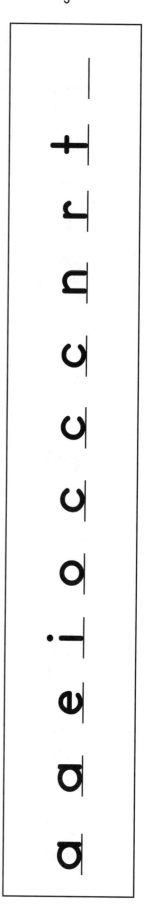

Making Places • CD-104108 • © Carson-Dellosa

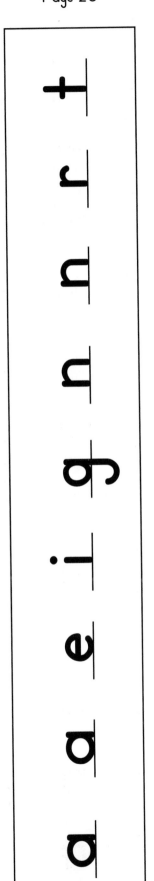

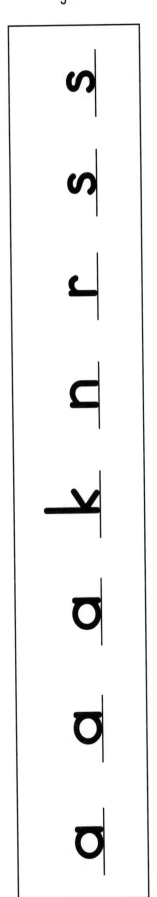

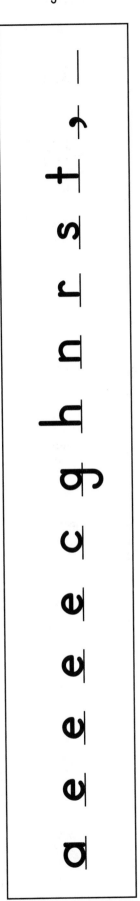

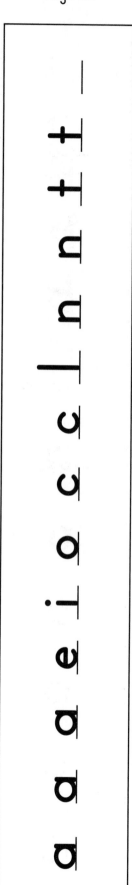

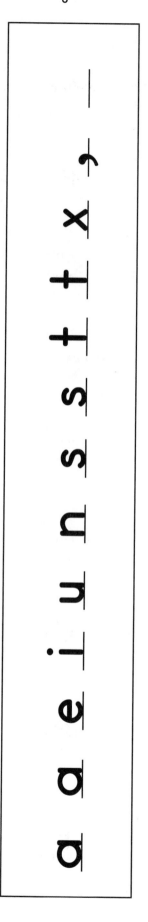

Page 26

a a a e i o c c l n n t t

Page 27

a a a e i u u g m n s t ’

Page 28

a a e i u n s s t t x ’

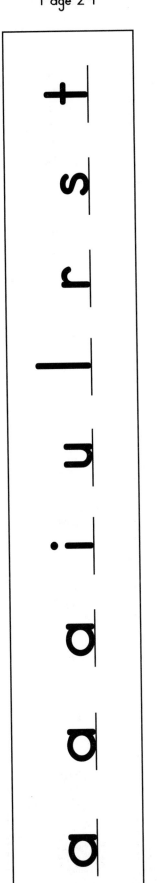

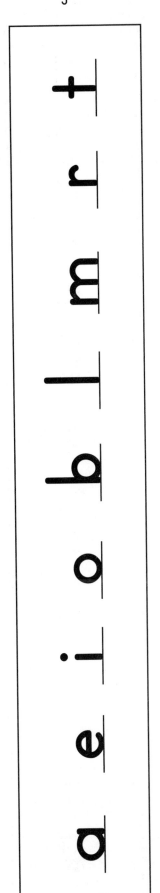

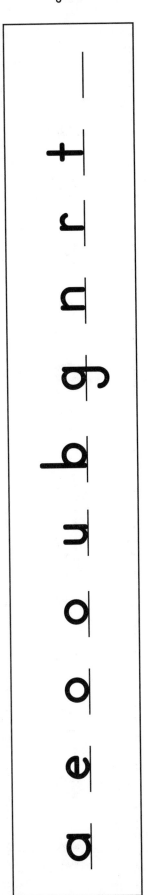

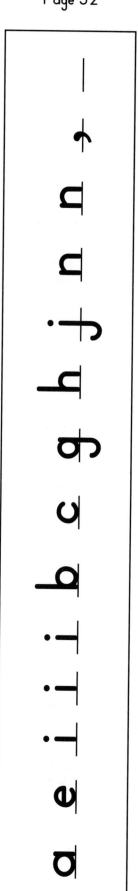

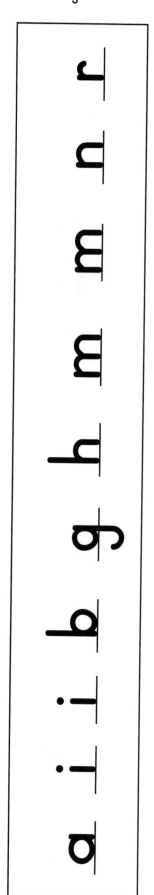

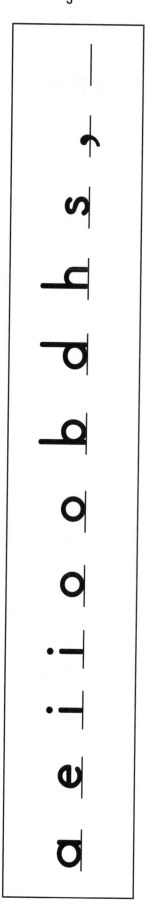

Making Places • CD-104108 • © Carson-Dellosa

Page 35   Page 36   Page 37

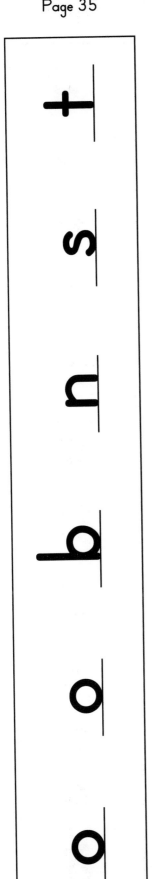

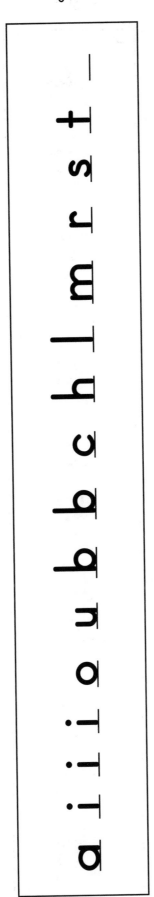

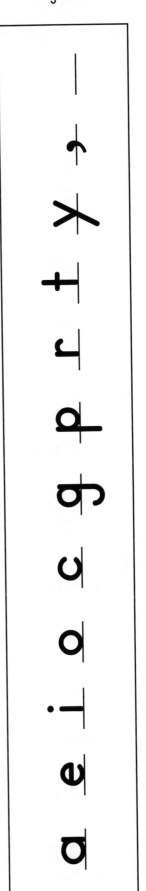

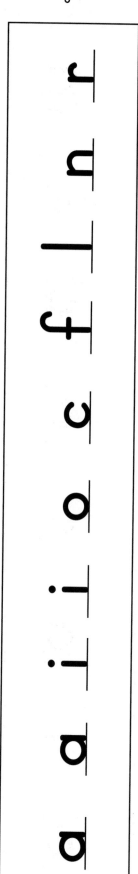

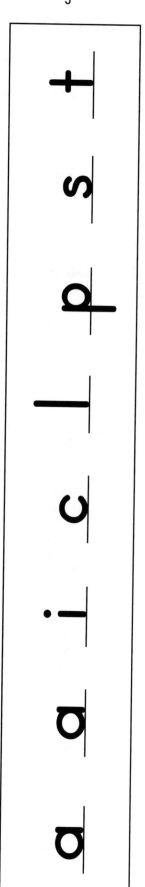

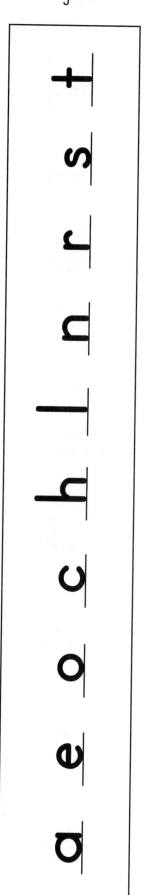

Making Places • CD-104108 • © Carson-Dellosa

Page 41: t t r l h h c o e a

Page 42: v n l l d c c e e a

Page 43: m l c b o o i a

Page 44: r l d c o o a

Page 45: s m l h c b u o o o i

Page 46: t t n n c c c u o i e

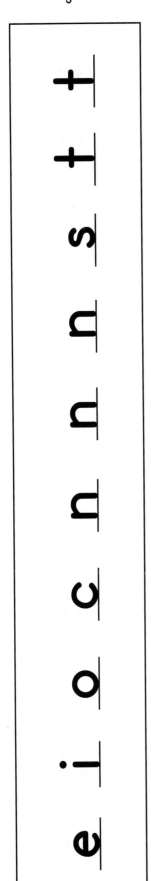

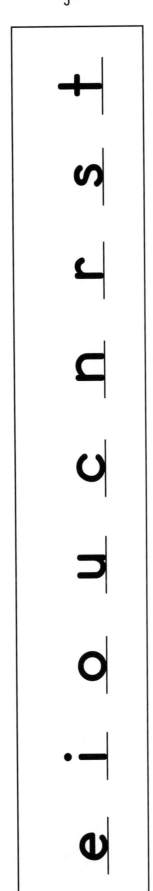

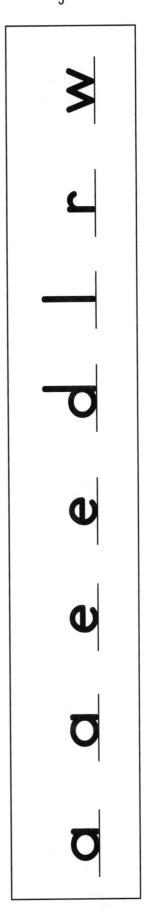

Page 50: r n m k d e a

Page 51: w s s n m d o o i i e e a

Page 52: t r h e a

Making Places • CD-104108 • © Carson-Dellosa

Page 53:

n u l g d e a

Page 54:

r l f p o i a

Page 55:

r g g o i e a

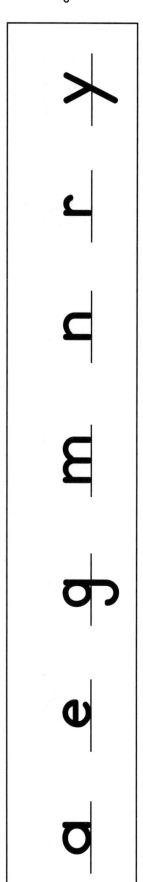

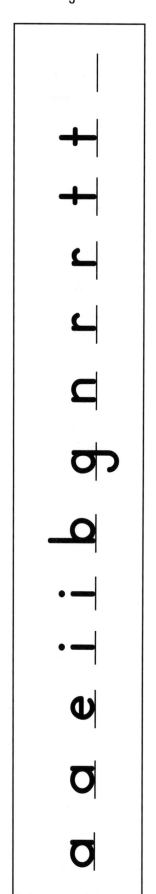

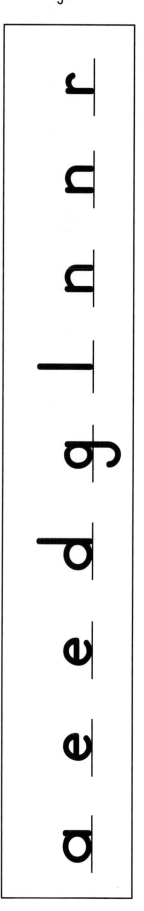

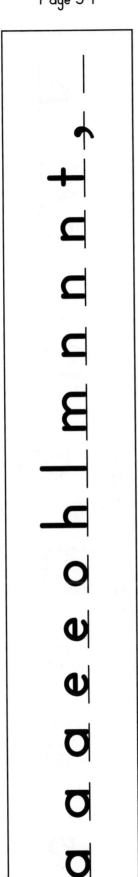

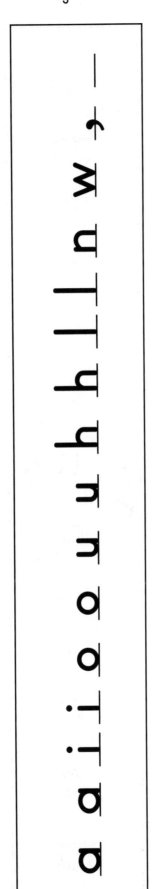

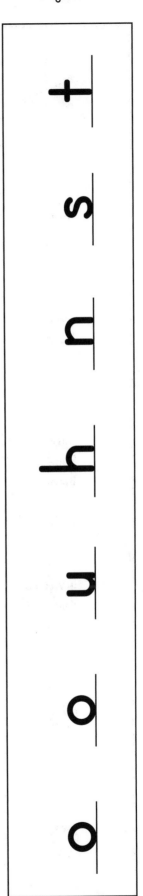

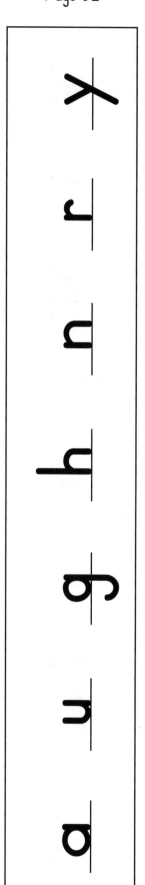
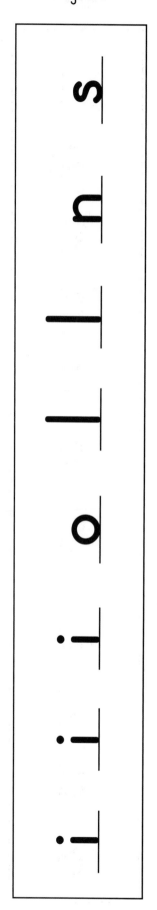
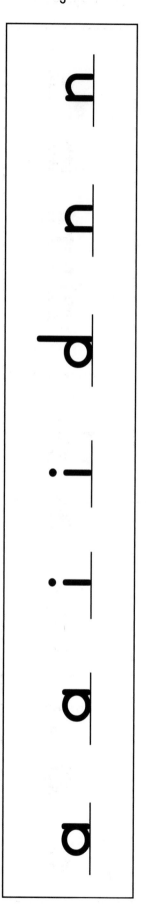

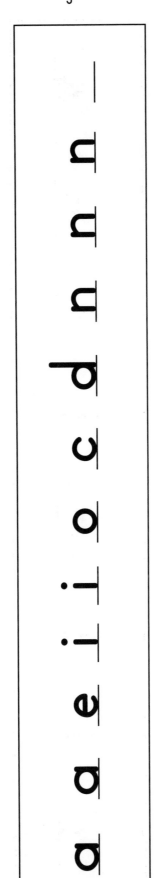

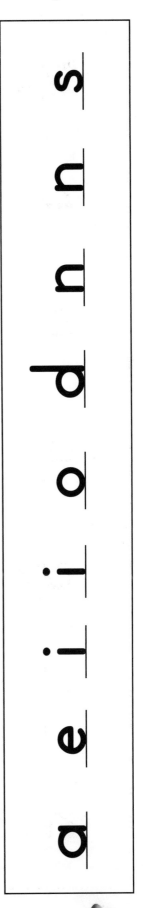

Page 68

r
n
l
d
i
e
a

Page 69

s
s
n
l
d
i
a

Page 70

s
r
l
i
e
a

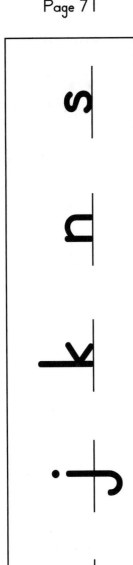

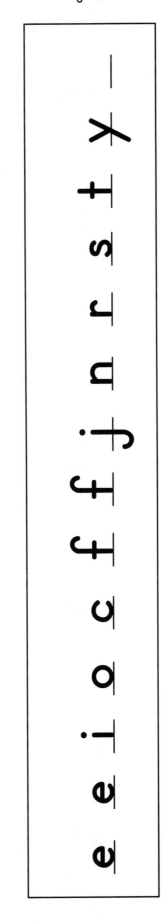

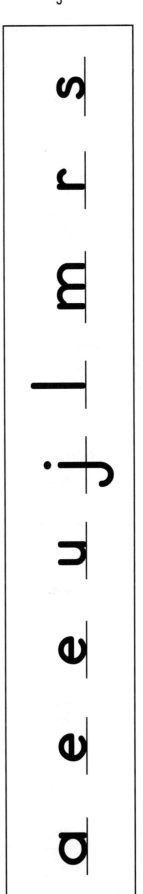

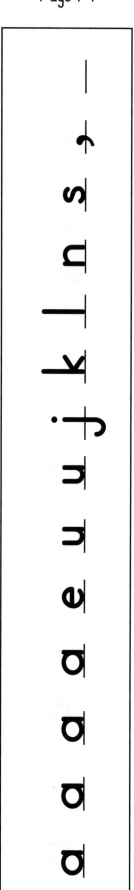

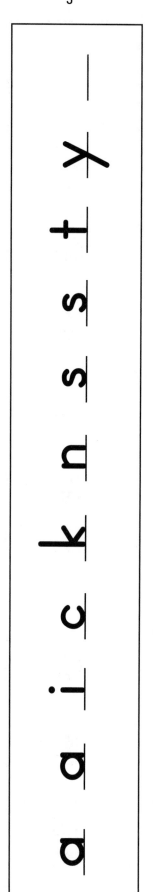

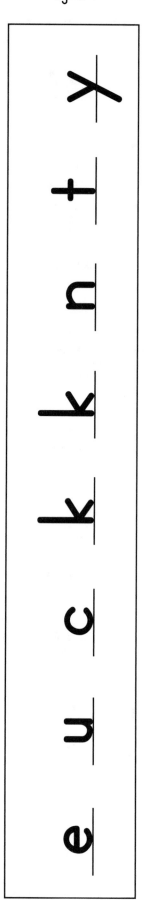

r l k i e e e a

r n k l l h u o e a

n m l k h g c i i e a a

a a e i o o k l n r t

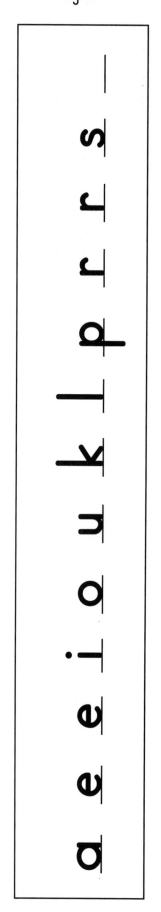

a e e i o u k l p r r s

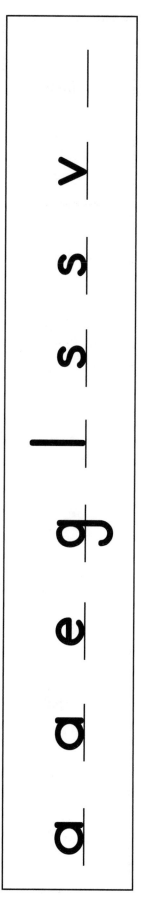

a a e g l s s v

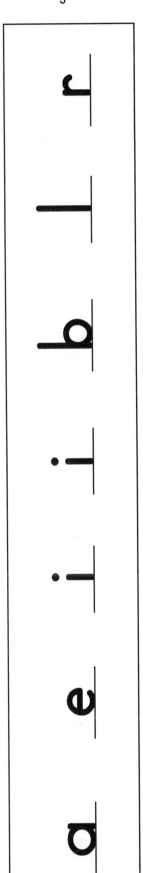

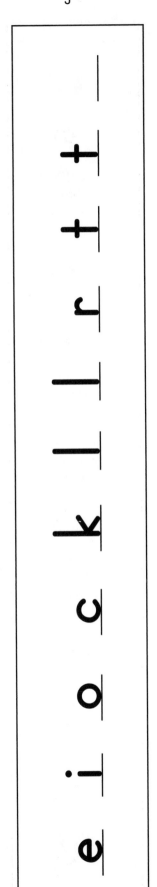

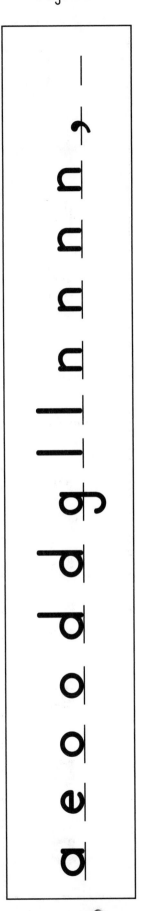

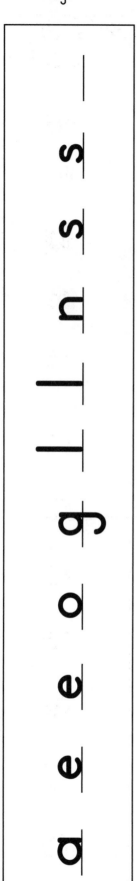

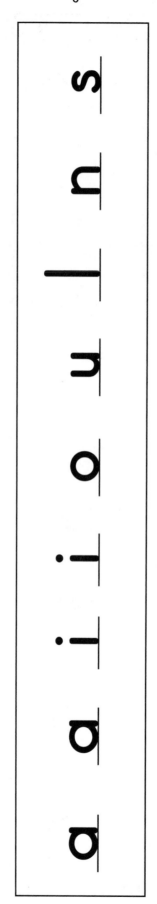

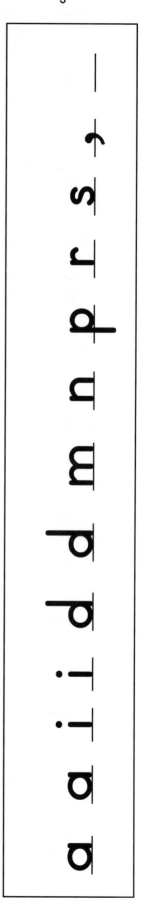

Making Places • CD-104108 • © Carson-Dellosa

Page 89   Page 90   Page 91

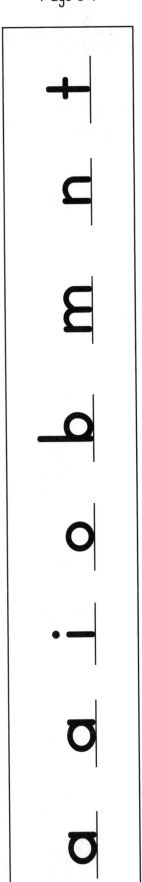

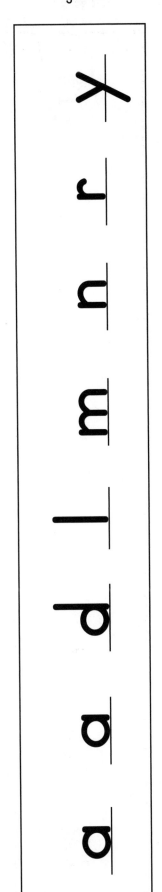

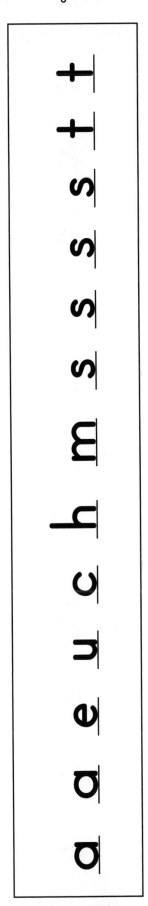

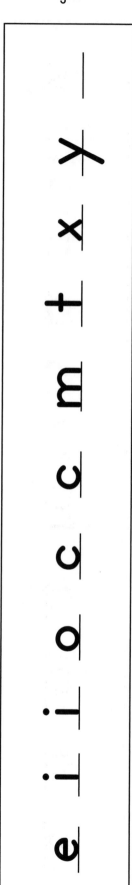

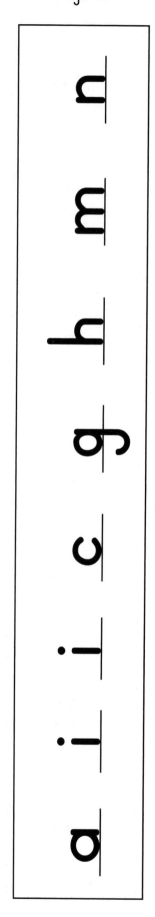

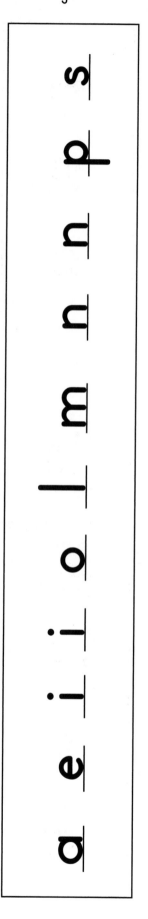

Making Places • CD-104108 • © Carson-Dellosa

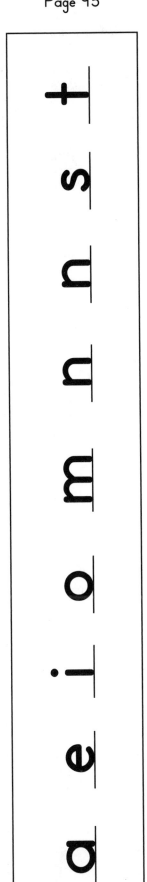

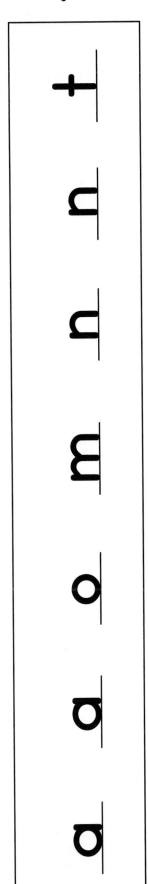

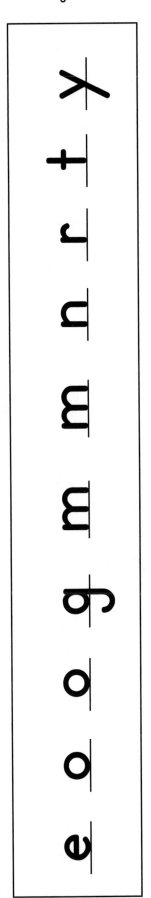

Page 98: t r n m l o e a

Page 99: w s s s r m c u o o i a

Page 100: t s n m u o i a

212

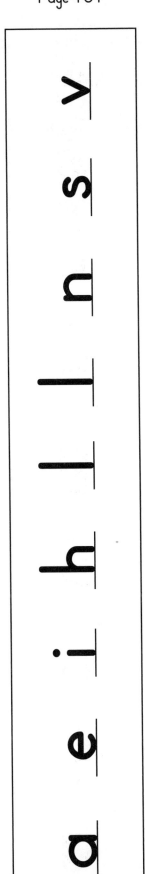
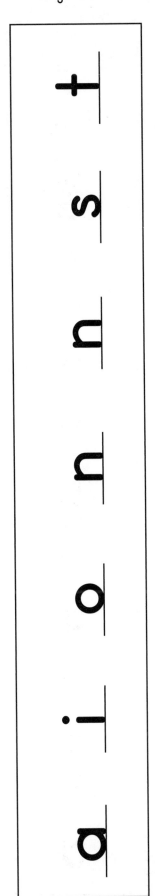
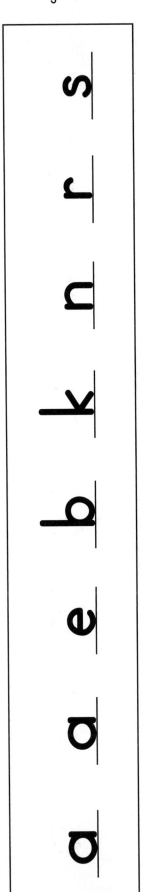

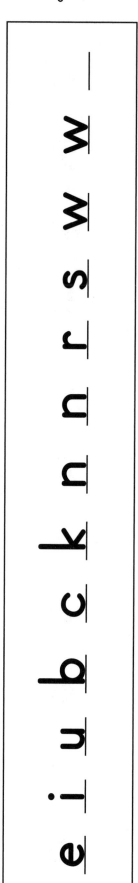

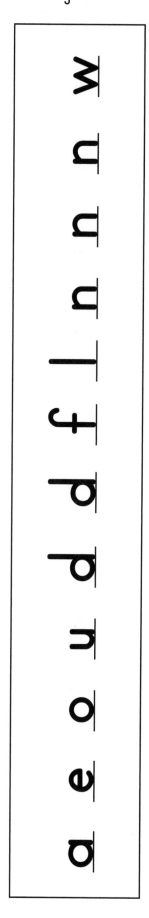

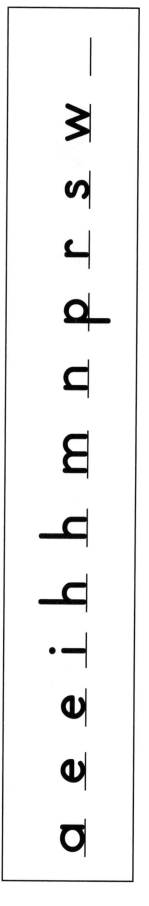

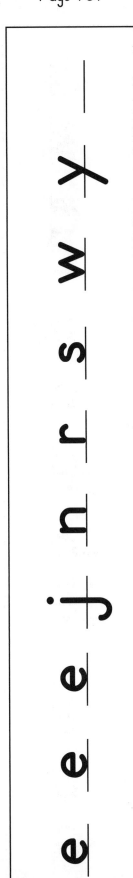

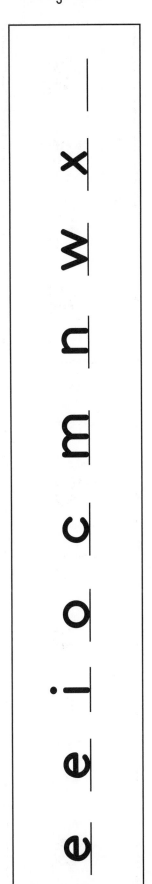

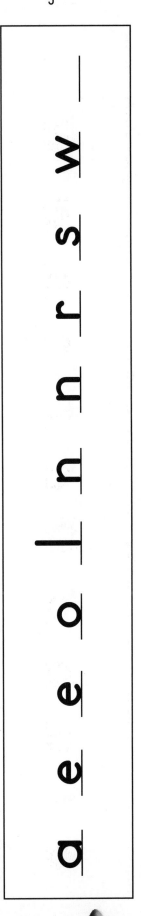

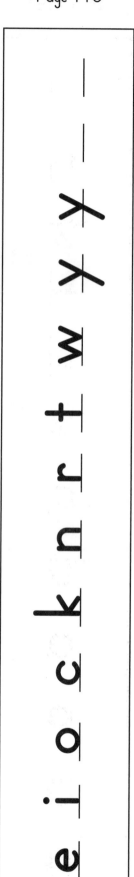
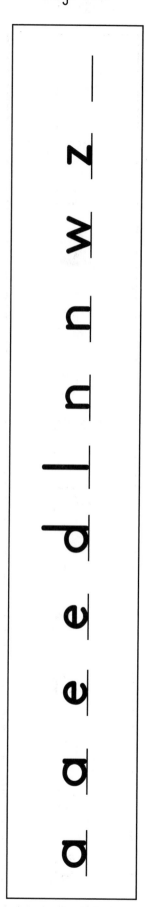
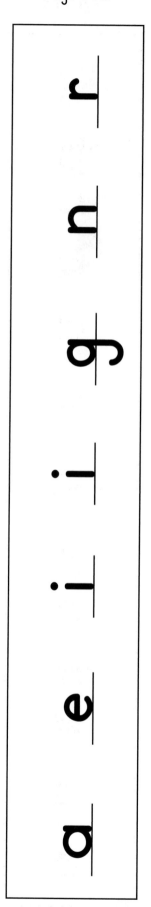

Making Places • CD-104108 • © Carson-Dellosa

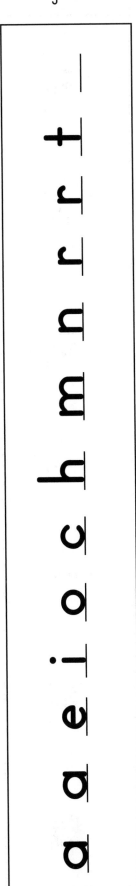

a a e i o c h m n r r t

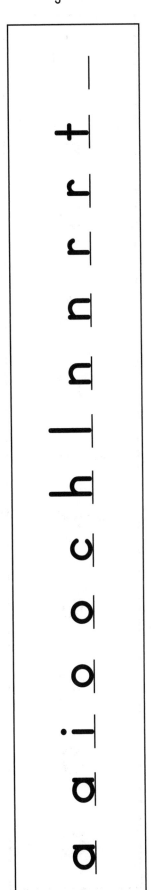

a a i o o c h l n n r r t

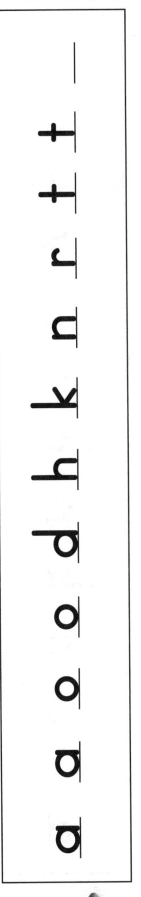

a a o o o d h h k n r t t

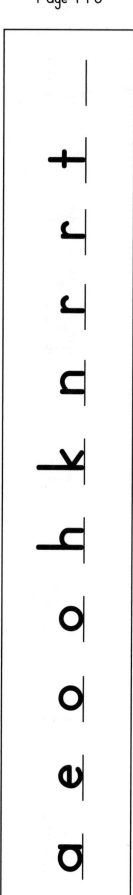

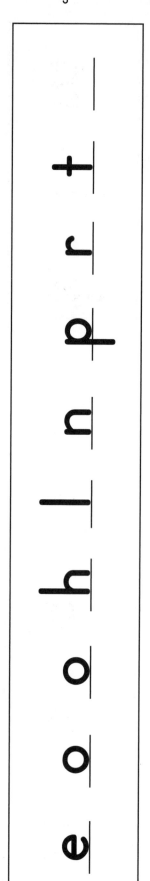

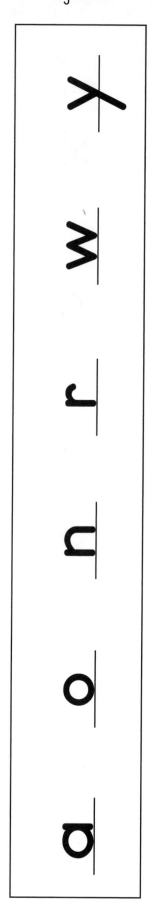

Making Places • CD-104108 • © Carson-Dellosa

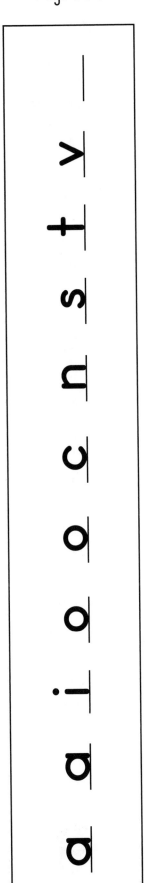

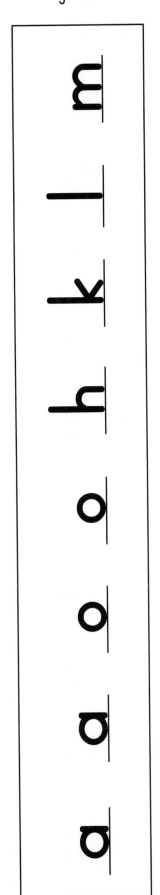

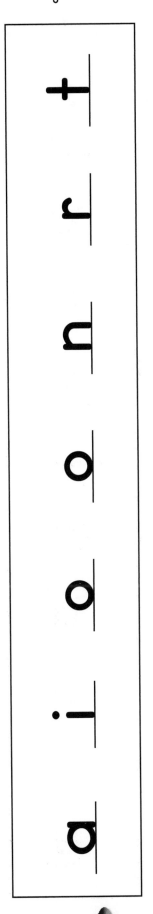

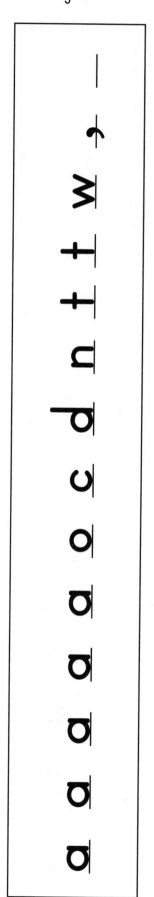

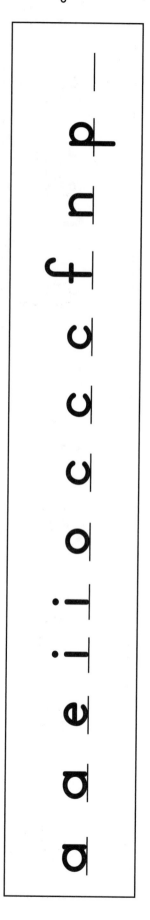

Making Places • CD-104108 • © Carson-Dellosa

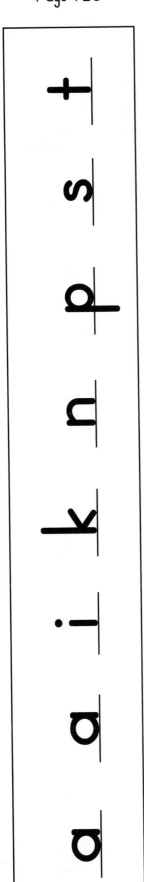

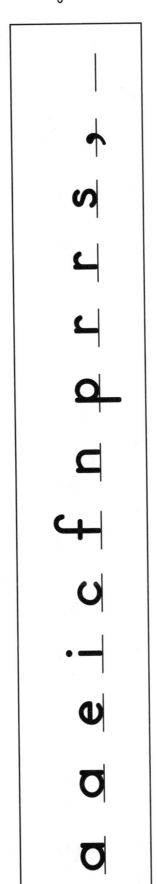

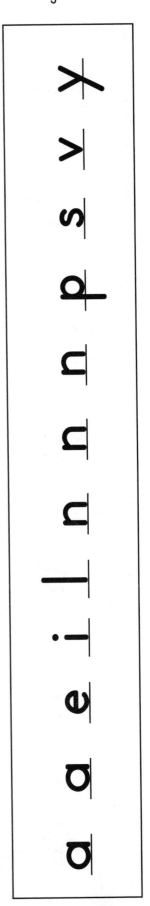

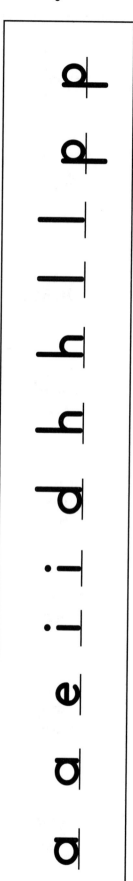

a a e i i d h h t l p p

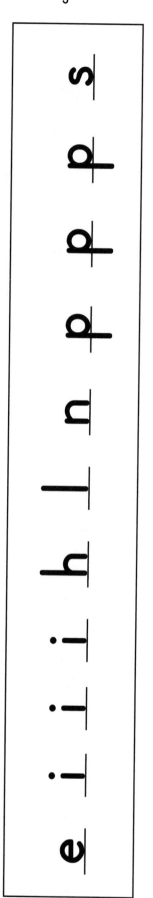

e i i i h l n p p s

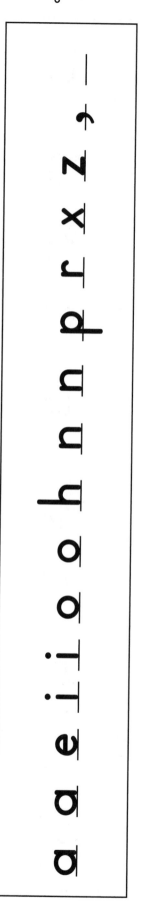

a a e i i o o h n n p r x z , —

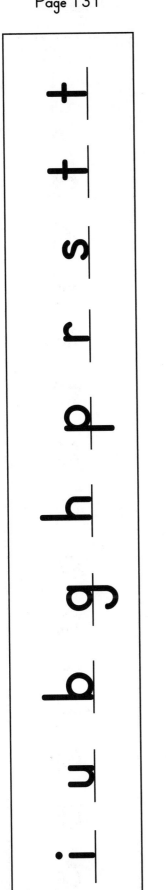

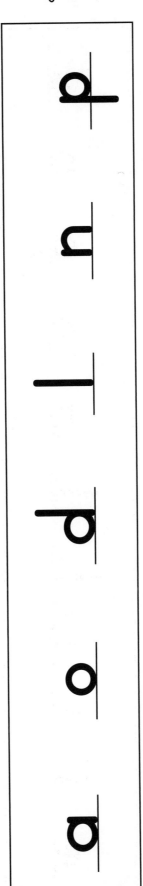

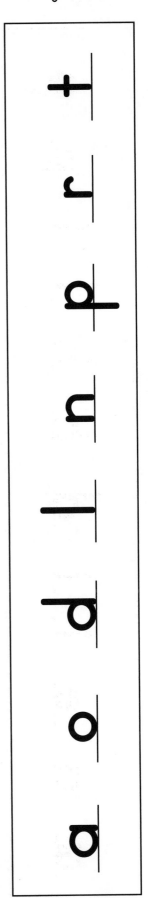

Page 134　　　　　Page 135　　　　　Page 136

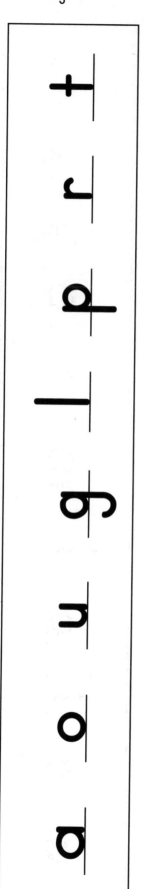

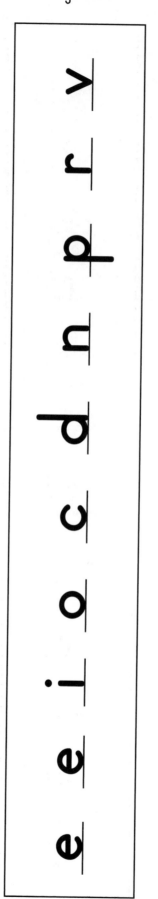

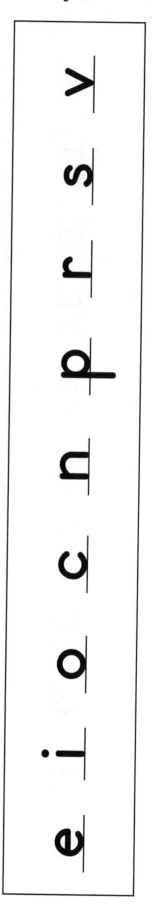

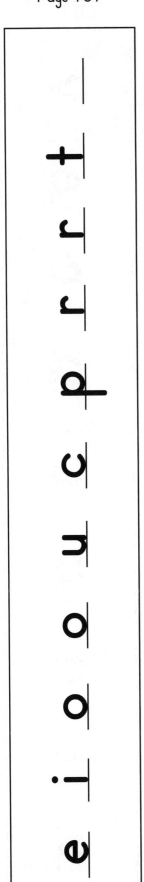

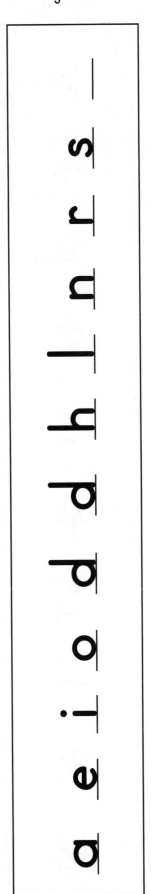

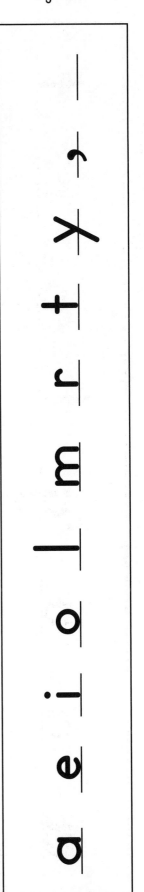

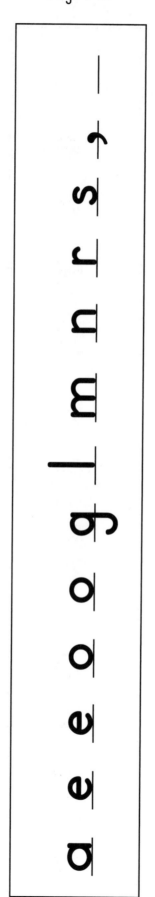

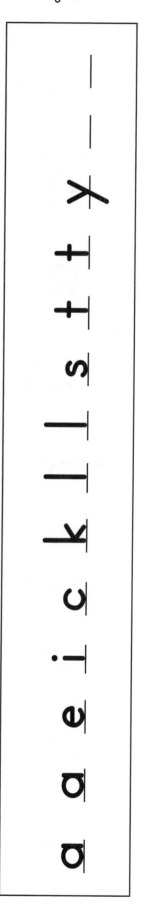

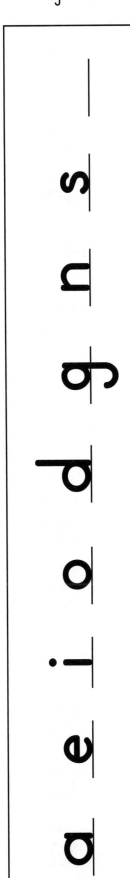

a e i o d g n s

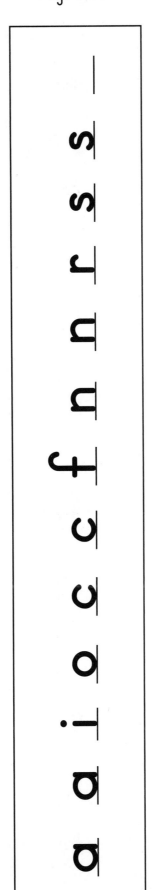

a a i o c c f n n r s s

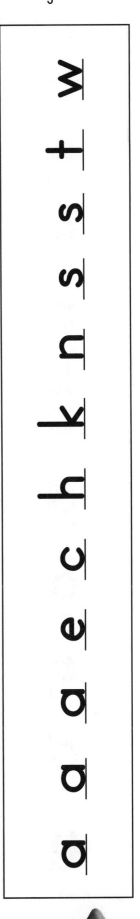

a a e c h k n s s t w

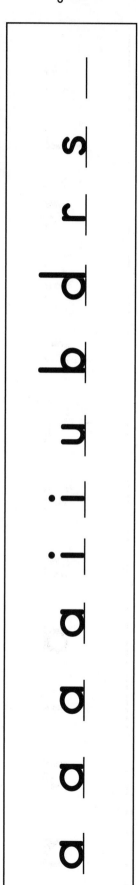
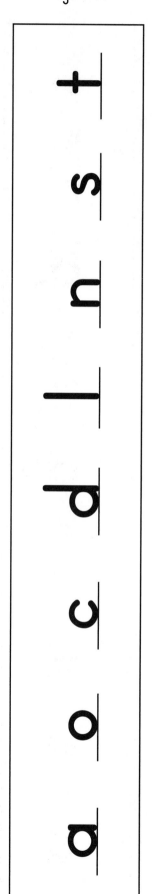
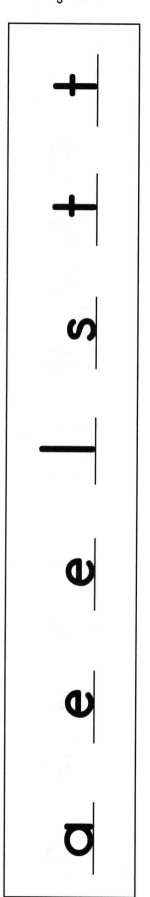

Making Places • CD-104108 • © Carson-Dellosa

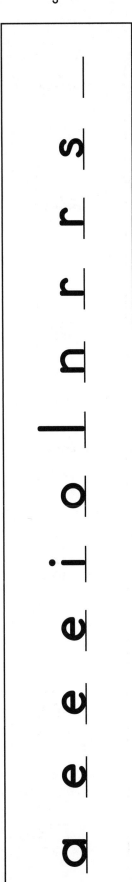

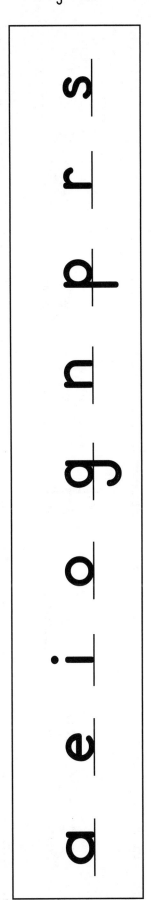

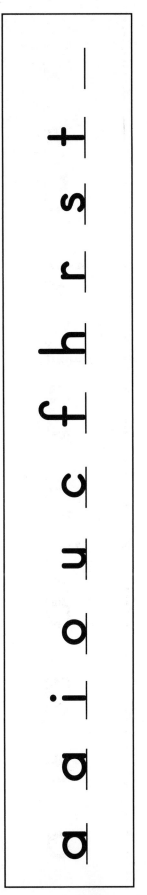

a a e i o u c h m r s t

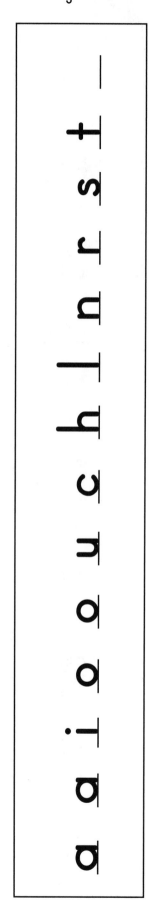

a a i o o u c h l n r s t

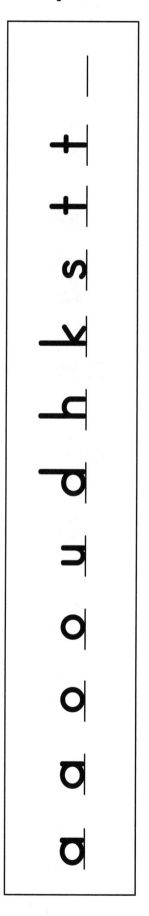

a a o o u d h h k s t t

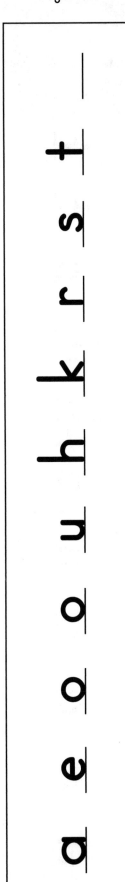

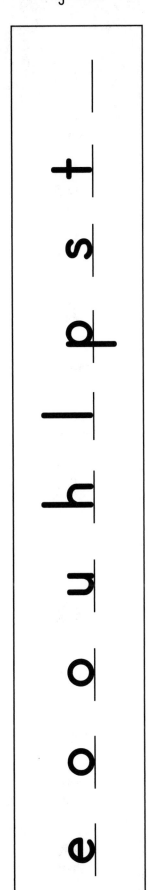

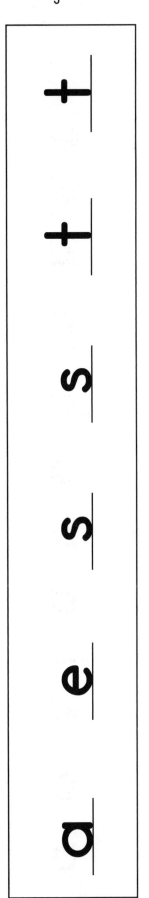

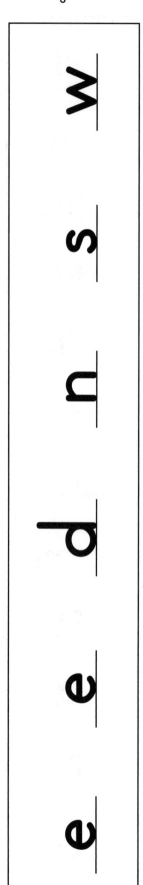

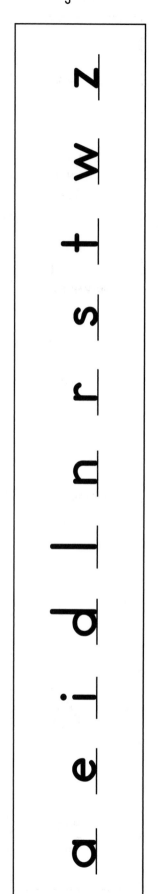

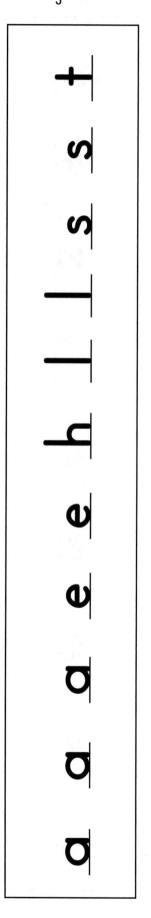

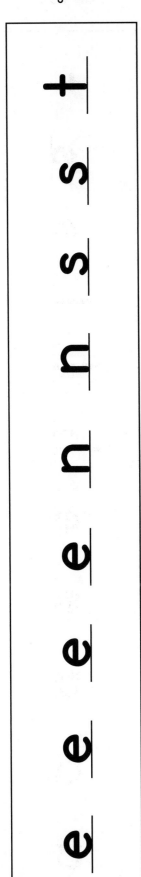

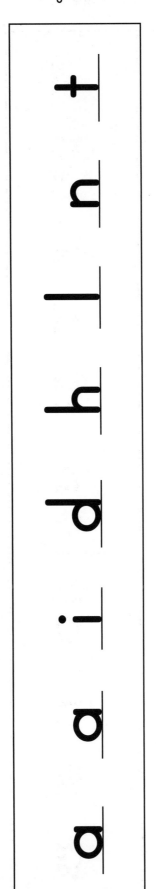

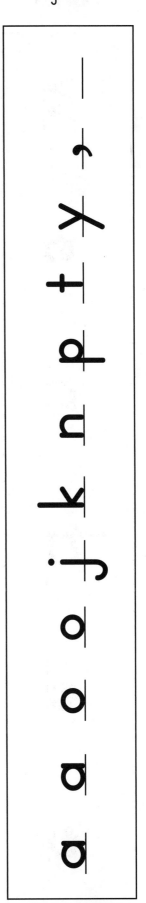

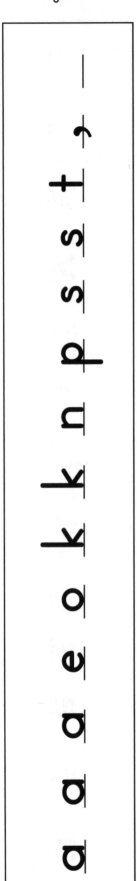

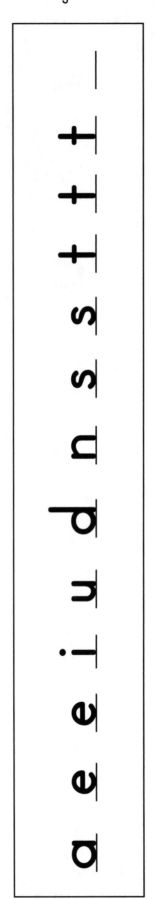

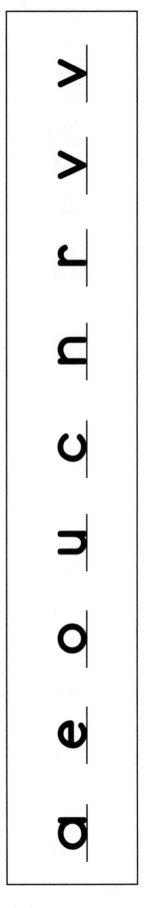

Making Places Take-Home Sheet

Cunningham, P. M. and Hall, D. P. (1994). *Making Words: Multilevel, Hands-On, Developmentally Appropriate Spelling and Phonics Activities*. Parsippany, NJ: Good Apple.